ASTROSOPHIC
PRINCIPLES
(1917)

An Enquiry into the Tenets and the Philosophy of the Stellar Science with Numerous Arguments, controversial and Evedentiary in support of its Rationality Including The Horoscope of Declaration of Independence Rectified from Historical Data and In Accordance with the /rules of Art.

John Hazelrigg

ISBN 1-56459-884-5

Request our FREE CATALOG of over 1,000
Rare Esoteric Books
<u>Unavailable Elsewhere</u>

Alchemy, Ancient Wisdom, Astronomy, Baconian, Eastern-Thought, Egyptology, Esoteric, Freemasonry, Gnosticism, Hermetic, Magic, Metaphysics, Mysticism, Mystery Schools, Mythology, Occult, Philosophy, Psychology, Pyramids, Qabalah, Religions, Rosicrucian, Science, Spiritual, Symbolism, Tarot, Theosophy, *and many more!*

Kessinger Publishing Company
Montana, U.S.A.

TO MY TWIN BROTHER

Oliver

On whom looked down at hour of birth
The galaxy of self-same stars,
Whence came the mirths and pains of earth
Dispensed by Heaven's Justicians—

**THIS BOOK IS AFFECTIONATELY DEDICATED
BY**
The Author

Aug 26, 1917

To Charley —
With the rest,
that is so highly treasured.
Your brother.
Oliver

ASTROSOPHIC PRINCIPLES

I

"And he denied him, saying, Woman, I know him not."—Luke xxii: 57.
"They said therefore unto him, Art thou not also one of his disciples? He denied it and said, I am not."—John xviii: 25.
"And he again denied with an oath, I do not know the man."—Matt. xxvi: 72.

THE Jewish conspiracy was not a marker as compared with the concert of hostility so unceasingly arrayed against the Messianic science of Astrology since the Biblical era. Adown the intervening centuries has trooped a blustering miscellany of repudiators, each trying to out-Peter his predecessor in the denial of that which, by order of Divine necessity, comprehends the very essence and the allness of his being. And, more's the pity, there is not one of them if asked to define Astrology would be capable of an intelligent reply; nor, for obvious reasons, to conceive the fact that, as every abjuration of the Christ principle is in effect a disavowal of the central law of Being itself, so must every calumny directed at this science be viewed as an attempt to discredit the true interpreter of that law.

It stands as a significant fact that not a single person has ever seriously examined into Astrology, willingly or otherwise, but with the ultimate conviction of its verity; and that every utterance in derogation of it has, without exception, come from sources devoid of a capacity to apprehend, obdurated by preconceptions, or else of too indolent a mental trend for conscientious inquiry into its tenets and its technicalities. To all such as these may be applied the sweeping assertion of one Bonus of Ferrara—"No one is really qualified to pass judgment upon any art or science who knows nothing about it"; and of Paracelsus—"No science can deservedly be held in contempt by one ignorant of its principles." And it may further be affirmed that no *right-minded* individual will presume to question the integrity of that which lies outside the pale of his seeking.

It is too often the habit of the conventional thinker to oppugn each and everything that happens to conflict with his mental diet, or that, perchance, eclipses his mental capabilities. That aught should dare exceed the vanishing point in the realm of his gray matter is to him the most arrant of presumptions, and to be berated with a blatancy suitable to the offense. It matters not that argument, to bear the stamp of honesty, must be fortified by technical familiarity with the subject at issue, and that, minus this, the only two weapons left him to do battle with, are the sophistical ones of obloquy and mudslinging. Being more expert in the manipulation of these than he is in apprehending the intellectual whereabouts of his adversary, he generally puts up a man of straw to his own liking, and proceeds forthwith to batter it down.

It would all be very humorous were it not so reprehensive, and yet to all thus afflicted by this form of mental egoism I would commend, as a balm to the outraged mind, the following statement of distinction:

To one is vouchsafed the idealism requisite for art, to another the brain potencies essential to mathematics, and yet to another the subtle processes which make for logic. And if the exponent of either of these stands related to the other two in a degree of ineptitude, it behooves that one, by all the laws of wisdom, to keep silent to the extent of his limitation; for antagonism, to be fruitful, must be directed by intelligence, and intelligence can by no manner of means ever be arrayed against truth.

That is why Astrology has for centuries survived the frown of the church, the heavy hand of the law, the contempt of the press, and the vilifications of others equally ignorant of its divine nature and its true relationship to natural law.

Had it been lacking in the essence of truth, it could not have shown itself possessed of so unparalleled a resistance. And though it may have passed from view for a while coincidentally with the recession of the Christ-spirit from out the hearts of men, it is only again to reappear upon the scene of humanity's trend towards the spiritual. Governments have risen and decayed; religions, reeking with cant and dogma, have upreared themselves, tottered and fallen; systems of thought have bowed in deference to newer concepts and fresher ideals, which in sequence have swayed and vanished with the turn of Time's kaleidoscope. Through it all this Bible of the Starry Heavens, whose story is woven with the woof of fact and whose characters personify the fundamental principles of an immutable Nature, has remained with unbroken text and design unaltered. "For certainly it is with art as it is with men, their age and continuance are good arguments of their strength and integrity."—*Thomas Vaughan.*

The being who imbibes a little of truth, and who, because of a porosity incapable of further absorption, immediately cries aloud in the frenzy of his conceit that he has it all and there is no more to be striven for, is very like unto the poor devil who stands shivering in his moral nakedness outside the vestibule; for his spiritual activities are still held in crystallization, and the warmth of receptivity has not as yet quickened the central fire of his soul. The really advanced thinker, the philosopher, is he who has no intellectual axe to grind, no prejudices to root out, who is broad enough for all truth in whatever guise it may come. Astrology appeals not in vain to such as he, for his breadth of purpose is an element most congenial to the mother economy whose laws he seeks to understand and expound.

Perhaps the most pitiable spectacle to contemplate is that of the mental egotist who unconsciously lives and teaches a principle which he ignorantly anathematizes; who incessantly harps upon the divinity of a Central Law, the essentiality of the atom to the molecule, the allness of Being and the consequent relationship of parts with a Whole—and then with chameleon-like cleverness proceeds to revile the interpretative system through which alone his statements may be intelligently proven. He has, as it were, stumbled blindly upon a cardinal fact, but there his capacity ends, his faculty of absorption is surfeited, and in his inability to turn the key that unlocks the combination of scientific spirituality and reveals the *law* of manifestation, he hoots instead of heeds. It was because of like treatment of the old alchemists that the moderns are such dullards in the science of spiritual chemistry.

I know not why I write in this defensive strain, for Truth has never yet found need of championship. But being a sensitive creature she rarely discloses herself to the individual who parades 'neath the cloak of Prejudice, and these sentiments may not go amiss as incentives to closer acquaintanceship with her on the part of him who would fain close the volume of knowledge ere the pages have been scanned.

This is an age of thought, and the time for downing facts by derision and testing truth by contumely has gone by; and unless the person to whom the above reference is made speedily aligns himself with the broad spirit of wisdom, he will shortly find himself in the pitiable plight of Peter at cockcrow.

II

The pomposity with which the general writer along scientific lines delivers himself of opinions when touching upon subjects of an occult character, reveals an erring tendency that is no less amazing than it is amusing. It is not to be gainsaid that his utterances are more frequently perversions than true statements of fact, for one must first have acquaintance with the premises of a subject ere he can hope to reason syllogistically. I have read and listened to many slurring phrases against Astrology, and without exception they one and all reek so of the murk of misconception that a mind even moderately informed on the question at issue must have marveled at the temerity which could have prompted them. One can, perhaps, overlook the animus of the astronomer, for naturally he does not fancy a relegation to rough-scullion duty in the back kitchen of Nature's establishment. But it is too much a habit of the scientific mind in general to dismiss with a sneer, or with misrepresentations, that which lies beyond his domain of effort; and, like the intellectual booby that he is—not having the frankness to admit his ignorance of any problem which Nature might happen to present—he awkwardly "puts his foot in it," without even so much as realizing the mishap. Yet he must grow sorely puzzled as he notes from time to time the wonderful re-discoveries being made along the very lines the mystics have been traversing throughout the ages. The period of denial is being rapidly replaced by an era of affirmation and the disciples of cold rationalism must speedily qualify for an apprehension of the inner mysteries, else remain as the toad, who from the depth of his marshy fastness perceives high aloft the circling curves made by the farther-viewing eaglet.

Time was when to acknowledge interest or belief in Astrology meant to arouse a storm of protest, or to be commiserated with for a fancied weakness in the intellectual region. But with the copious outflow of the spirit of inquiry now manifesting in the minds of the masses, a degree of familiarity with the principles involved is deemed as equally a *sine qua non* to its intelligent consideration as is similarly exacted in the discussion of other subjects. No longer does a reference to the doctrine elicit such responses as "Nonsense!" "Too silly for serious thought!" etc. Instead comes the more honest and conservative answer, "I don't know," or "I haven't inquired into it." This is progress, the receptive stage that precedes conviction; the condition wherein one is willing, if not inclined to personal investigation, at least to concede intelligence to the one who has thus directed his mental energies, and to defer to that one's more capable and reliable judgment. It is only the conceited ass who assumes to speak authoritatively of matters with which he is even less than tentatively concerned; opinion rightfully belongs only to him whose interrogative tastes have led him in the direction of the searcher's goal.

Some years ago the Rev. T. DeWitt Talmage delivered a Christmas sermon in which he touched upon a few of the significant facts attending the mission of the Wise Men into Bethlehem, and of the character of these Wise Men he said:

"The Wise Men of the East came to Christ. They were not fools, they were not imbeciles. The record distinctly says that the Wise Men came to Christ. We say they were the magi, or they were the alchemists, or they were the astrologers, and we say it with depreciating accentuation. Why, they were the most splendid and magnificent men of the century. They were the naturalists and the scientists. They knew all that was known. You must remember that astrology was the mother of astronomy, and that alchemy was the mother of chemistry. It was the life-long business of these astrologers to study the stars. Twenty-two hundred and fifty years before Christ was born the wise men knew the precession of the equinoxes, and they had calculated the orbits and the returns of the comets. We find in the book of Job that the men of olden time did not suppose the world was flat, as some have said, but that he knew, and the men of his time knew, the world was globular. The pyramids were built for astrological and astronomical study. Then, the alchemists spent their lives in the study of metals and gases, and liquids, and solids, and in filling the world's library with their wonderful discoveries. They were vastly wise men who came to the East. *After the world has gone on studying hundreds of years it may come up to the point where the ancients began to forget."*

III

It is gratifying to note the growing intelligence and credibility with which Astrology is now being received, for there is no exaggeration in the statement that of all the sciences none has been so lightly inquired into, so woefully misunderstood, or so maliciously maligned as this. It is but fair to state that Astrology is no more exempt from charlatanism than are the multiple of other callings. Medicine is accorded respect in spite of the uncertainty and quackery which conventionalizes it; law is given servility notwithstanding the shysterism, the malfeasance and the injustice practiced in its name, while the Church exacts a blind adherence in face of the weakness and duplicity of its teachers. Individual shortcomings harm neither of these. But Astrology, the noblest of them all, needs be held accountable for the peccadilloes and assumptions of spurious practitioners who fatten on the credulity of the supplicant that has turned aside from the insufficiencies of Church and State in search of a more practical solution to the problems of his life. The lay mind may perceive its absolute verity without necessarily being familiar with its technicalities. One is not required to study medical law to apprehend a rationalistic truth in the healing art; one need not be familiar with astronomy to know it as a branch of higher mathematics; neither is it needful to be able to cast a horoscope in order to recognize in Astrology a system of celestial dynamics by which finite mind may interpret the bent of the eternal verities, whether they incline to the physical, the spiritual, or the ethical sides of nature.

The materialist, necessarily restricted in his concepts, has a thriving habit of ascribing to superstition any fact outside the pale of concrete logic. He can recognize no magic potency in the creative thought which directs the involving processes of a universe: he sees only what nature has externalized. To him the slight deviation from the fiat of the physicist is rank apostasy, and a belief in aught which deals with the activities of a supersensual plane as a working hypothesis, is "superstition." The delvers and the believers in Astrology have not escaped the odium intended in this charge. For centuries this science has received the gibes of the bigoted and been belabored with the cudgels of the intolerant, either of which class is either too prejudiced to inquire into, or too obtuse to assimilate, its truths. And yet in a term meant to be opprobrious these contemners unwittingly pay tribute to the higher percipiency of the mystic temperament, for what does "superstition" imply other than a rising out of limited confines into the broad domains of greater heights? As we all know, the word itself is derived from *super,* above, and from the root of the verb *sto,* to stand, meaning literally "to stand above." If in the interest of truth to rise above a crystallized condition of narrow-mindedness is to be superstitious, then say we, All hail to distinction!

In the farther East, the fount and locale of magic and mysticism, of religion and the astral sciences, the horoscopes of all infants are calculated at birth, and marital unions, arranged at an early age, are based upon the sympathy existent in the respective nativities. Needless to say, the divorce court is an unknown institution in those countries. Such a system of domestic economics may seem incongruous with our idea of "free choice," though the latter is usually but another name for a haphazard selection which more often results in anything but freedom. This is illustrated every day in our Western civilization, where Cupid runs riot with a companion god called Convenience, utterly heedless of the consequent admixture of hostile temperaments. Dissimilar elements, when arranged in juxtaposition, must tend unalterably to discord, if not chaos. "Knowledge is power," and in no part of nature is it so essential as in the direction of human destiny. The intelligent study and application of astrologic science will mean mental and physical rejuvenation for the race, a healthier spiritual attunement, and a clearer apprehension of fundamental truth as it is, and not as it is supposed to be.

With a recognition of the ego as a part of the All comes naturally the inquiry as to its individual status in relation to that All. We feel justified in saying that through no scientific means can this be so accurately determined as by the horoscope, or figure of the heavens, at birth, and from whence alone may be reckoned the mental, the moral, and the physical *tendencies* and capabilities of the incarnated ego. Only through a proper apprehension of these, such as a horoscope affords, can the after processes of elimination or development be intelligently carried forward. As this fact of a relative individualism becomes better known, the infant will be conceded an importance independent of family heredity or parental absolutism, and Astrology will be accorded its rightful value as *the* basic factor in the science of stirpiculture.

IV

The astrologer is often asked, if his art be true why is it not accorded more popular recognition? Why is it the least known of all branches of learning? Why is the scientific world so persistently arrayed against it? To the first and second of these questions it will suffice to state that the art is of too subtle and abstruse a character to admit of a general familiarity with its hypotheses and complexities. While all other departments of learning are each crowded with thousands of its especial votaries, only a very small percentage of the scientifically inclined are by temperament fitted to go beyond physical limits in their nature-journeys; so, in the enforced recognition of this fact the "scientist" is left no other alternative than to rail against the object of his discomfiture. It is a way the human animal has of squaring himself against unpleasant amenities. This answers the third question, in connection with which we have some further comment to offer. A system that deals only with matter cannot hope to comprehend the astral subtilties, and the devotee who accustoms himself to view the operations of nature only from the phenomenal standpoint, will be forever incapable of grasping the truth which steals cunningly along the highway which leads from Cause to Effect. No blame ever attaches to an individual for lack of special qualifications in any given channel; condemnation belongs only to him who seeks to destroy that which he has neither the capacity nor the honesty to examine. To this class belonged those scientists who refused to peer through Galileo's telescope lest they be converted to a belief in his newly-discovered fact; and of the same ilk are these modern scientists who are afflicted with a like intellectual cowardice in respect to Astrology. But of all such as cannot yet conceive of its verity, be they apathetics or contemners, we would comfort with the assurance that the inward light of the stars is fast dawning upon the world, and sooner or later every individual will become possessed in an increasing degree of the higher perceptions which appertain to a universal racial development; and to ye that cannot understand, Astrology says as said Jesus to Peter: "Whither I go thou canst not follow me now, but *thou shalt follow me afterwards!*"

Because of the comparative silence of Astrology for a great number of years, it became the fond belief of the mentally timid and the conventionally minded—those enamored of dogma and artificiality—that it had lapsed into a desuetude quite too eternal for resurrection. Some there were who even boasted that "science" had knocked it into a cocked hat, by such impact exploding it into smithereens. But because a cloud has momentarily obscured the light of the Sun, is it any reason to believe that the central luminary has gone out of business? No more can Truth be suspected of withholding permanently one ray of its effulgence from the glory of the world. Only a casual glance adown the corridors of time is necessary to note the persistency with which this spiritual searchlight periodically illumines the human journey. Astrology is the same yesterday, to-day and forever, though humanity, impelled by a recessional law along the under arc of its evolution, may for a time lose consciousness of its divinity—albeit the beacon be still shining from the opposite zenith—and so believe it to have totally vanished from mortal ken. But anon we come once again to the horizon, and behold! there in the heavens still shines the Star of Interpretation, doubtless somewhat strange to us because of the enforced separation, but none the less scintillant in its majesty and grandeur. Racially, humanity is once again touching this rising point in its circle of motion, hence the recrudescence of interest in the theme of the stars, and in all that concerns the spiritual weal of the body politic.

V

There are two people to whom the world looks for infallibility, though with a differing degree of exaction—the Pope and the astrologer. With no intentional irreverence towards the Sage of the Vatican, I think I may safely assert that the one is about as omniscient as the other. Human judgment, whether fortified by temporal acquirements or through spiritual knowledge, is subject to limitations, and to err is one of its enforced privileges. In spite of this fact, however, there is a prevalency in the minds of many to jump heavily upon the poor prophet the instant his tired brain fails correctly to grasp the complexities with which he deals, and he is immediately stamped a pretender, or else his science is anathematized as having no basis in truth. But let a physician make a mistake in diagnosis, or err in the line of treatment, does it mean ostracism for him, or a denial of the laws with which he deals? Church canons undergo periodical revision, necessitating new interpretations and a new adjustment to the ethics involved, but the question of a previous infallibility in regard to them is faithfully lost sight of in the rapture of a new devotion. How different it has been with the astrologer who dared to misjudge the immutable, unvarying laws of this beautiful, universal Nature that admits neither of change nor amendment! In some countries they have been accustomed to chop his head off for so unpardonable an offense, though in later times our more civilized communities have resorted to the more refined cruelty of holding him up to obloquy, a pariah to be shunned of all men. But times are changing, and if he still, in a measure, clings to the common prerogative to err, I am glad to find the world is at last learning to view his occasional mistakes with the same charity it accords to others similarly circumstanced.

These problems of preordination and fatalism have cried out for solution ever since man first viewed the starry heavens as the intermediary source of the various determinations which make up the sum and substance of his existence. That the lesser must co-ordinate in character with the greater, is fundamentally necessary if extremes are to meet to form the complete circle of being. And as long as man is subject to associations, whether in a sense of competition or co-operation—as long as he stands inter-related with the component parts of a universal whole, just so long must he continue an integral factor in the general scheme, and therefore be subject to the forces revolving in and throughout the same. After a varied experience in practical Astrology, I certainly find it difficult to conceive of any operation in a natal figure as failing to impress itself, except some contravening element placed there by the progenitive power stands in the way of its expression; and if such there be it may be found so recorded, if one will but look closely enough and in the right place. If, as saith the platitudinarian, "the wise man rules his stars, the fool obeys them,"— as is so often droned misunderstandingly by upholders of the astral doctrine,—then one must conclude that the world is sadly lacking in wisdom, and that humanity in the aggregate is composed of very foolish parts. And yet there is truth in the axiom, even though its application be possible in only a very few isolated instances; for Man Regenerate, he in whom divine order has been restored, in whom the astral centers have regained their proper places about the God-center of his being—such an one, through the law of attainment, is no longer subject to sidereal influx. But how many have reached to this condition of divinity since the Christ doctrine was first enunciated æons agone? So very, very few that we may consistently continue to search our horoscopes for the probable happenings of the future, with a pretty sure certainty that directional arcs will continue to culminate with their customary degree of pertinency. Henri Frederic Amiel wrote years ago in his *Journal Intime:* "Man may give himself what trouble he will—God leads him all the same." And God is still leading us, through celestial realms and adown stellar pathways, as He has been doing since the lights were first placed in the firmament "for signs and for seasons."

VI

Astrology is essentially a doctrine of correspondences, based upon the proposition of a necessary interaction between the component parts of a universe whose primal law is one of unity. Its rationality may therefore be said to abide in a self-evident truth. It may reasonably be conceded the greatest antiquity of any branch of learning, being coeval with the earliest civilizations of which we have any account. Prior to the middle ages it embraced that part of sidereal physics designated as Astronomy. This latter, as now circumscribed, treats of the *body*, the material or physical aspect of the empyrean, while Astrology has to do with its *soul*, or the transcendental phases which accord to it life and meaning. It is therefore to be viewed as one of the three major divisions in the Doctrine of Nature, of which it is the link between the lower and the higher, viz.: Astronomy (body), Astrology (soul), Alchemy (spirit).

It comprehends a science, an art, and a philosophy, in which respect it may be regarded as a trinity in unity.

1st. As a science it elucidates the truth of fundamental principles co-existing between a world of cause and a world of effect, relative planes of manifestation specified respectively as

(a) The *Macrocosm*, which is the great Universe from whence emanate the astral potencies as physicalized in the planetary orbs; and
(b) The *Microcosm*, or the universe in miniature, as applied to the organism of the human monad. The ancients conceived the internal man as being formed to the image of heaven, hence termed him a microcosm. Astrology scientifically proves the identity of the two.

2nd. As an art it involves the faculty of interpretation, of the ability to prejudge the logical ultimate to a definite chain of causes, such as may be indicated in a series of aspects in process of formation between the celestial arbiters. Such faculty may be denominated *Prescience*, which is born of the active union of intellect with intuition, and without which one cannot hope to enter successfully into the realms of scientific prophecy. The term is peculiarly apposite to a system of interpretation such as Astrology, that recognizes the oneness of Nature and the fact of a mutual dependency between the higher and the lower.

3rd. As a philosophy it assumes that the varying qualities in the human temperament, whether sensible or essential, are natural sequences to antecedent impulses to which the individual bears an unconscious relationship; therefore not to be gauged from the standpoint of personal responsibility, but in the light of Divine necessity. As Herbert Spencer says—"There can be no correct idea of a part without a correct idea of the correlative whole. . . . And again, the position which the part occupies in relation to other parts cannot be rightly conceived unless there is some conception of the whole." This statement may readily serve as the corner-stone of ethical astrology, for only in clearly apprehending the *causes* of so-called inequalities in the human family, as revealed through this knowledge of the correlations in nature, can undesirable tendencies be eliminated and an adjustment in the moral economy of the individual be intelligently striven for.

This trinity thus cursorily presented merges into and is characteristically a part of that branch of the stellar science known as Genethialogy, in which the problems of life and destiny are deduced from a figure of the heavens calculated for the time and place of birth, and in consonance with the observed analogies existing between the celestial and terrestrial planes of manifestation. The horoscope thus supplies the psychic key to that of which the infant, in its projection into nominal selfhood, is a reflex or copy: just as if one were to separate a drop from a measure of discolored or otherwise medicated water, the drop would be of a like character with that from which it is taken, though subsequent manipulation may purify or alter its complexion. Now, the infant is as a drop from out the ocean of the universe, and, as such, is chemically identical with that ocean at the time of its extraction. This is the natural insistence of that law of harmony which is necessary for a sustained relationship between the parts of the whole. Hence, the propriety of observing the constitution of the heavens at the natal moment.

The reality and rationale of sidereal influence are vested in the universal law of Sympathy—the coactive factor in all relationship, physical and superphysical. "Every atom of matter, as a concrete expression of spiritual energy, answers to a keynote in the scale of Universal Being, and is endowed with a magnetic responsiveness in perfect accord with certain activities which constitute the Divine harmony. This theory finds an apt illustration in the intervibratory action of equivalent strings in different musical instruments placed in the same room, when a string in one has been set in motion—a recognized phenomenon in experimental physics."—*Metaphysical Astrology*. As with the musical instruments, the planets (psychical centres) in man, the microcosm, must and do respond to those in the Macrocosm when mutually and geometrically related, and that through a psycho-vibratory law beyond the grasp of the finite mind fully to comprehend. The solution is suggested but not explained by the underlying principles of wireless telegraphy.

These points, thus merely touched upon, will acquaint the investigator with certain facts essential to an initial grasp of a very erudite subject, and thus serve as a foundation upon which to rear the superstructure of his belief, and as irrefutable arguments for the "faith within him."

1. Let us have now a little practical chat on Astrology and see if we can't strike up a more familiar acquaintance with the subject.

The relationship between the stars and mundane matters should be comparatively easy of comprehension and acceptance. One need only admit the inseparableness of the All, the ubiquity of the One Law, and he will have grasped the fundamental idea in which reposes the Doctrine of the Stars.

Can one imagine a grander or more comprehensive starting-point?

2. The interaction between the planets and man is but the sympathies of the universe in activity. And let it here be said that the term "planets," as understood in the astral science, indicates "planes of activity," of which the celestial bodies, as outward manifestations, are merely symbols. They represent the seven basic principles in the Creative Economy which we find expressed in every organized instance of being. Our bodies are made up of the same elements which constitute the solar system; in fact, as individuals we are universes in miniature. You have this pictured in part in your family almanacs in the figure of the man, with the twelve signs of the zodiac circumjacent to the parts governed. Did you ever before view yourself from so stupendous a vantage ground? or realize that your feelings or your emotions were as the lulls, the calms, the storms, or the tempests, which characterize the elements about you?

3. To better understand the interdependence of these principles as scientifically related to the Mother Soul, one may find their counterparts in every department of universal nature, as evidenced in the few following analogies between the celestial orbs and sublunary phenomena:

Sun	Moon	Mercury	Venus	Mars	Jupiter	Saturn
Re	Fa	Si	Mi	Do	La	Sol
Gold	Silver	Mercury	Copper	Iron	Tin	Lead
Orange	Green	Violet	Yellow	Red	Indigo	Blue
Heart	Brain	Lungs	Reins	Gall	Liver	Spleen
R. Eye	L. Eye	Speech	Feeling	Smell	Taste	Hearing
Spirit	Soul	Intellect	Love	Energy	Judgment	Memory

These are but different manifestations of the same vibratory law, found expressed through the mystic seven on all planes of activity, whether it be in the sidereal heavens, in the world of metals, in music, in color, or in the human functions. And as the pure white ray of light is synthetic of all the prismatic colors—as shown by spectrum analysis—so does every one of the seven principles contain a ratio of the other six.

Nature works through a system of respondence and correspondence, of which Astrology is the interpretative science.

4. As before intimated, man is possessed of a sidereal organism whose operations accord with the mutations in the ambient. Thus, when Saturn is afflicted by contrary aspects in the heavens a diverse temper of the atmosphere may be expected; when he is ill-conditioned in a horoscope the spleen becomes disordered, coinciding with a case of the "blues." When Mars aspects the luminaries in the solar system, calorific influences send the thermometer up; if he afflict the Sun or Moon in the individual constitution, red or inflammatory conditions result; if he afflict Jupiter the liver is affected, and the biliary ducts become obstructed. Is it any wonder that Hippocrates, the "father of medicine," should have said, "A physician is incompetent to practice physic if he be unacquainted with astrology"?

5. It will thus be seen that when we speak of Jupiter, of Saturn, or of the other planets, we do not attach an importance to them as merely conglobate bodies moving in space, but refer rather to the principles of which they as symbols are the manifestations. They are gigantic batteries from which irradiate the creative energies, and have not within themselves the element of causation: as the combination of zinc and copper does not *create* the electricity generated thereby, but only brings to a point of individualization that which is everywhere existent. And so when Jupiter comes to an aspect of Venus (copper) the conditions, as in the metals referred to above, have been formed for an efflux of the celestial magnetism in quality and degree according to the polarities which these planets possess at the time of such combination.

Does Astrology begin to look to you more rational and scientific than you had formerly supposed?

For many, many centuries the science has been anathematized because misunderstood. But we propose to clear away some of the cobwebs that have gathered because of this stricture and neglect, and to prove to you that our universe has a *soul*, and that the lesser souls *must* and *do* respond in conscious vibration with the outworking of the general plan.

6. B. G. Jenkins, F.R.A.S., of England, in an article published in *The Pall Mall Gazette*, London, says:

"The reasons why people of the present day do not believe in planetary influence are two-fold—first, it is held to betoken ignorance and superstition; points on which educated people are very sensitive, and secondly, they cannot imagine how such tiny objects can affect their great globe, unconsciously forgetting that our earth among the planets is as a pea among cannon balls. From a lengthy study of this subject, I can come to no other conclusion than that the planets of the solar system are intimately connected with the phenomena or what takes place on this earth, and I shall, in as few words as possible, lay before the reader my reasons for such a conclusion."

Also from the same article is the following:

"From the lofty heights of modern science we have been accustomed to look down with pity and contempt upon the Astrologers of the Middle Ages—the weak dabblers in science, who were foolish enough to believe that the stars had an influence upon man. An allusion to Astrology was always good to raise a laugh at a science meeting, and the Astrologers and Alchemists were classed together as either dreamers or charlatans. Of late years, however, a reaction has set in. The Astrologer is becoming habilitated very rapidly. The influence of the planets upon the earth is now admitted to be very distinct, and fresh proofs of their disturbing influences are constantly cropping out."

Astrosophic Principles

In a previous paragraph I spoke of the analogies in nature, the similitudes between principle and planet. That these are not mere coincidences—a term, by the way, known only to the pseudo-scientist—I have every reason to believe will be easy of demonstration.

7. Take the seven colors, for instance, and let's see wherein they harmonize with other functions in nature. Newton inclined to the theory that these were all primitive, but later experiments in this field of physics by Ray, Field, Brewster, *et al.*, reduced this number to three—red, yellow and blue, called the primary colors, of which the other four are but combinations, and termed secondaries. They hereby touched the keynote of Nature's Trinity, that wonderful process through and by which all her manifold objects are attained. These represent the three properties of the sun ray, as illustrated in the adjoining diagram, extending from the violet (actinism, spring) through the yellow (light, summer) down to the red (heat, autumn, or ripening season).

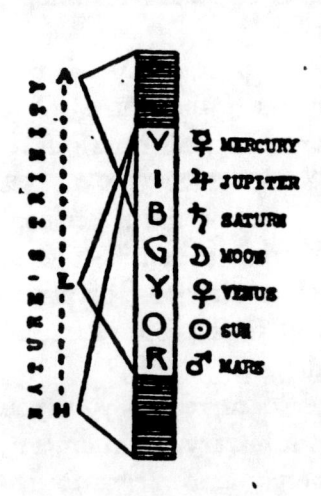

Any good work on solar physics will explain these facts *in extenso*. I need only add that *Nature never deviates from this method*, whether it apply to the lower kingdom of plant life, the comprehensive organism of a larger universe, or the intellectual fructification of a human thought. As principles all the planets, all the colors, all the various degrees of vibratory force, are inexorably represented; and in the seven centres of the physiological system the same order obtains, as expressed in harmony with the twelve body constellations or functional planes of activity.

8. The trinal division of the spectrum, as referred to above, is the basis of every religion the world has ever known, revealing the three-fold process of that universal God of Nature, equally as important in the Brahma, Vishnu, and Siva of the Hindu as in the Father, Son and Holy Ghost of the nominal Christian. The alchemist embodied it in his Mercury, Sulphur, and Salt, while the School of the Mystics called it Spirit, Soul and Body, or cause, action and effect, and represented by the Circle (O), Crescent ( )) and Cross (+). Look at those planetary symbols above, and see if a ray of light doesn't begin to dawn on you. Do you begin to perceive wherein theological dogma abstracted itself from the Sun or Astrological religion, and then turned around and denied its paternity?

Do you now wonder why Aristotle should have so wisely averred that there were "four noble sciences—Astrology, Physics, Magic and Alchemy"?

9. The Circle was used to represent Spirit, because it was without beginning and without end; this is the Sun symbol, with the primal point of manifestation indicated in its centre. The Crescent was the reflection or Soul, which you can see any time at night when the Moon is receding from her conjunction with the Sun, the negative acting as a reflective to the positive. The Cross typified the four elements, or planes of material activities, found in astrology in the four elemental divisions, called triplicities, of the zodiac.

10. No doubt if the thought ever occurred to you, you judged these symbols to be purely arbitrary in character, quaint little curly-ma-cues adopted merely as a means to distinguish one planet from the other. But to prove that they have a deeper significance, take, for instance, Venus, in astrology the Goddess of Love. Note that the circle, or pure spirit, surmounts the cross. Now compare it with the symbol of Mars, the God of War, and you will see that material

conflict and desire is dominant over spirit. Venus being love is the unifying principle in nature, and you will find her in the above diagram as the center of Light (yellow), the greatest point of intensity in the spectrum. She represents that period of the season when Nature bursts forth with a song of joy and thanksgiving in anticipation of the ripening or full fruition of her purposes.

11. As further evidence of the astrological root from which sprang the tree of celestial symbolism, one need only compare the Jupiter and Saturn characters—as found in our diagram—in relation to their occult significance. In the former it will be observed that the crescent precedes the cross, for the soul principle which it represents is dominant over the material instincts. Did you ever know a jovial (Jupiter) nature that did not abound in soul qualities, exuberant with the generous impulses which make for the milk of human kindness?

In the saturnine individual the reverse side of the man medal is shown, just as in the symbol of that planet the material glyph is found overshadowing the crescent of the soul. And so does the saturnine being partake of the negative qualities of the blue ray, which superinduces to melancholy, austerity, and such like tendencies as beget cold, suspicion, orthodoxy and selfishness. The miser, the ritualist, the devotee to time-honored custom and ceremony, has the Saturn element in the ascendency at the time of his nativity, and unbends but grudgingly to the inevitableness of evolutionary progress; while the spendthrift, the hale-fellow-well-met, the humanitarian, the believer in the eternal verities and the goodness of God, is an out-and-out Jupiterian, absorbing the indigo principle of spiritual oxygen with every inhalation that stirs the activities of his being.

12. Astrology is the only science that affords a practical key to these inner mysteries, and he who anathematizes it

seeks to revile that Father of Nature of whom he is the legitimate though misguided offspring.

In the investigation of an *astrologia sana*, such as was taught by the mystics, one must recognize the ubiquity of that all pervading essence from which are generated not only the cosmic life forces, but from out the centre of which is diffused the vivifying light of transcendental truth. He who alienates himself from this grandeur of spiritual perception through a selfish adherence to an illusive materiality, builds up a stone wall to obscure his vision and shut from his sight the beauties of the scene beyond.

VIII

13. By a previous reference to the septenary divisions in mundane nature as analogous to the seven planets, it was sought to impress upon the mind the fact of a distinct series of vibrations uniform on every plane of the Universal Consciousness.

"As is the highest, so is the lowest." This maxim is the essential starting point in astrology, which seeks through its tenets to establish the homogeneity of these seven creative principles, and to define their values as related to material form. Physical science, in dealing with effects rather than causes, directs its scrutiny at the external side of things only, and placing its bony digital at the point of observation, pompously declares, "It is here, or not at all!" Is it any wonder that, as with the ever-changing methods of the materialist, it should generally be "not at all"? To seek Truth outside the domain of Cause would be like traversing the vascular system in search of the human soul, or attempting to see God through a telescope.

But where, you ask, is this domain of Cause? I answer, *you are part and parcel of it*, you are the whole alphabet of its language, its seven principles which are as the seven planets, not circumscribed by a terrestrial condition, but the synthesis of the heavens above and round about you to the very confines of illimitable space itself!

14. Paracelsus states:—"As the world is within itself an organism with all its constellations, so is man a constellation, a world in himself. . . . . This firmament in man has its planets and stars, its exaltations, conjunctions and oppositions. . . . His heart is his Sun, his brain his Moon, the spleen his Saturn, the liver Jupiter, the lungs Mercury, and his kidneys, Venus.". Do you begin to scent the full significance of the scriptural assertion that you are formed in the image of God —which is Nature? Remember I am now referring to principles, or facts, and not to man-made creeds or dogmas. The "God within" statement finds no logical scientific demonstration outside the doctrine of Astrology, which teaches that the heaven within is prototypal of the heavens above, and that these different planes (planets) of spiritual activity, in relation to the problem of all life, are as the unknown or algebraic quantities through which mathematical truth is discerned.

15. The ancient philosophers, but relatively concerned with the externalities to be viewed by the physical eye, sought rather for the *soul* of things; and being spiritually cognizant of the seven principles, they easily attained to a knowledge of fundamental truth through methods of metaphysical induction and the law of correspondence, going forward from the cause rather than backward from the effect. He who follows the latter course usually brings up against a stone wall, and being

unable to see on the other side he is pretty willing to swear there is no other side. Such is the result of having reasoned in a straight line instead of embracing the whole circle in the range of one's logic.

16. Bacon, a professed votary of the astral science, is said to have invented this inductive system of thought, to which Astrology owes its discovery and development. One might invent form, but not idea, and the learned Bacon, in his perambulations through the realms of the higher philosophy, wisely followed the analytical processes of his predecessors.

Thales of Miletus, Pythagoras of Samos, and Hippocrates of Chios, all astrologers, schooled in the inductive method of reasoning, were thus enabled to introduce propositions which subsequently were utilized by Euclid in the formation of his Elements; Galileo, accustomed to deal with abstract principle as elucidated in his beloved study of the stars, gave to us the telescope, as well as the discovery of the moon's diurnal and monthly librations: Newton, a student of Astrology, through his indefatigable delving into the *cause* of things, laid bare the principle of gravitation: and Kepler, also an astrologer, was inductively led into the discovery of the elliptical revolutions of the planets, embraced in his three laws which "constitute almost the sum of astronomical knowledge."

And these were the avowed advocates of a science which other branches of philosophy have of late years deemed "unworthy of notice." Obviously merit is not proof against ostracism.

And here may we lament the fact that never since astronomy disunited itself from Astrology, its mother and *soul*, has there been any new discovery of facts in astral mathematics equalling the above in fundamental importance. Having disavowed their obligations to the paternal teachings as recognized by the above intellectual worthies, one must regard the contemners of Astrology as about equally incapable of attaining to these concepts as Weary Waggles would be of appreciating the culinary virtues of a Perigord pie.

IX

17. The Eternal Scribe, when writing his signature across the face of the Heavens, made use of no uncertain or arbitrary characters, for, as with man-made idioms, the alphabet of Nature has its consonants, its vowels, and its diphthongs, a reality which is at once poetical and capable of being logically demonstrated. There is a spiritual principle, or transcendent *cause,* back of every manifestation in the external world of *effect,* just as oral speech is but the expression of precedent thought. "God thought, and man was." All tongues necessarily have a common origin and purpose because identical with the universal language of the stars, of which the seven planets are the vowels, the twelve zodiacal signs are the consonants, and Uranus and Neptune—the octave expressions of Mercury and Venus—are the diphthongs. The sibilants, the gutturals, and the aspirates comport with the interstellar spaces that are as relative impulses in the eduction of physical form.

18. These facts, though doubtless strange to many of you, were incorporated in the teachings of the Mystics away back in the Night of Time. And he who can to-day read nature in the light of this language has the power to sense about him a keynote to every thought of the Divine Mind; for every rock, every plant, every tree, while responding in partial degree to every vibratory value indicated in this celestial al-

phabet, must, through the very nature of its individual constitution, harmonize more fully with one particular letter, sign, planet. Such is the dictum of that law of sympathy, of harmony, of relationship, of mutual dependence, of attraction and gravitation which is essential to order in a universe of constant activity.

Herein lies the rationale of Astrology in its contention that each part and each fraction of a part in Nature's organism is related specifically to other parts, of which the stars and zodiacal signs are but representative principles analogous to those which fill every conceivable point in space.

19. It was through centuries of observation and inductive reasoning on the part of the ancient Magi that the fundamental values between the component parts of the universe were psychically discerned and mathematically verified, and the interpretative system of Astrology thereby firmly established. This was the work of seers to whom the kindergarten blocks in the astral scheme meant something more than merely objects at which to train a telescope. The physical scientist who can perceive naught in truth beyond its externalization into opaque form, is not temperamentally adapted to this kind of research. To him Venus has no significance outside her physical constitution or her velocity through space; to the metaphysico-astral student she moves majestically through the boundless ether as the embodiment of a *principle* which inheres in every constituent part of Nature's *spiritual* structure.

There is no avenue in scientific exploration more fruitful of wisdom than is afforded by a study of the similitudes in this grand scheme of which we are a part, confirming as it does the existence of a law of interactions operative between the celestial and corporeal worlds.

20. As in dynamics there is a positive and a negative pole, so in astral physics do we find *sympathy* and *antipathy* expressed as polar opposites of the one law. Therefore, when

planets contrary in temperament come into astronomical aspect, or, astrologically, into magnetic relationship, with each other, disturbances ensue in forms which stand constitutionally related thereto. For instance, Saturn as the symbol of cold negation, is antipathetic to the Sun, the dynamic principle of heat, expansion. Hence, when the former comes into correlative terms with the latter in the zodiac the temperature is lowered and the aqueous vapor in the atmosphere is condensed. Watch your almanac and note when this aspect occurs again, and you will agree with this fact which has been recognized by the astrologer ever since man became a percipient being. And so will an equivalent condition be noted when Saturn in the heavens throws an evil ray to the place of the Sun in the individual horoscope, depleting the life forces as well as affecting the material interests. Mix blue (Saturn) and orange (Sun) colors together, and you have the same inharmonious result on a different functional plane.

21. And so do the letters in this mysterious alphabet of Nature often so shape themselves in the kingdom of Cause as to spell havoc, and misery and destruction to the lesser forces which mark the commas, the periods and the exclamation points in the domain of Effect; though anon they tell a tale of love, of benignancy, and of happy fruition to the hopes and the aspirations which go soaring from mortal mind throughout the realms of star dust in tuneful harmony with the music of the spheres.

For the study of nature must ever lead up to Nature's God.

X.

22. In contemplating the marvelous superstructure of Astrology, reared as it is upon a system of mathematical equations, the question of a fixed destiny in human affairs inevitably presents itself to the mind of the student. He reasons with himself, that as certain impulses, as planetary arcs, are in process of formation at birth, and which must at a specified time culminate in results agreeably to the nature of the celestial arbiters concerned, does not such imply an indissoluble connection of cause with effect, and therefore a predetermination which can neither be hastened nor hindered?

23. I confess the proposition seems to admit only of an affirmative reply. And yet, accustomed as the individual is to regard himself as an independent agent, he very naturally protests against any hypothesis which subjects him to plans other than his own, though by so doing he lose sight of the fact that in universals there can be no self-hood; that "every whole is greater than its parts;" that to profess the capability to wield arbitrary control over even an infinitesimal fraction of Nature's organon, is to claim dominion over the ONE LAW in which reposes the idea of Unity.

24. To the astrologer as an observer of these interesting by-plays in the game of destiny, there is afforded cumulative proof that man, whether he wills it or not, is amenable to his astral environment, and as an aliquot part of the divine problem he must ever co-ordinate with the mathematical processes in operation at his birth. *He can neither create, erase, nor destroy a single ordinance in the book of Nature.* Could he do so he would be as the Infinite itself, and might with equal plausibility fashion a universe to his own liking.

25. Mind, I do not say that he may not, through an intel-

ligent apprehension of the celestial purposes, so bring himself into harmony with the general outworking as to function along the lines of least resistance; but yet he does not alter one iota the predestined intentions as revealed at the moment of his nativity. Thus, if Saturn be afflicted in his second house, and he thereby be incapable of attracting material riches, he may yet develop a contentment in poverty that will mean greater wealth to him than are the hoarded millions to the miser. Again he has not changed a law, but by adapting himself to its exigencies he becomes happy in the enjoyment of a kindred affluence. Therefore, who dare assert that a Morgan, a Gould, or a Rockefeller is wealthier than he? But if the stars have not made a philosopher of him, I fear me indigence of soul as well as body will be his lot.

26. How often one plods along at an uncertain gait, running amuck with every imaginable obstacle which can obtrude itself, when all at once a clever idea germinates in his brain which brings success, and he wonders, "Why did I not think of this years before, and so have escaped all these struggles?" Yes, why not? Because his thinking faculties lacked the necessary lubricant until nature, with her mysterious methods of adjustment, so stimulated the brain with the astral fluid as to engender a clearer and more logical thought action.

27. It would be all very well for such an one to credit his success to his own unaided efforts; but the astrologer knows that only a very limited achievement is possible with Mercury in conjunction with Saturn and the luminaries afflicted, for such would so cloud the perceptions that the chance of a lifetime would pass well beyond the reach before its import could be grasped; or else lower the attractive quality to such an extent as to repel the favors of fortune. On the other hand, the man with Mercury in good aspect with the Sun, Moon, and Mars and a fiery or fixed sign rising, seldom lets an opportunity escape his clutch.

Is this fate? Is it destiny? If not, what name shall we give to these commensurables that are carefully measured out in quantities varying with the horoscopical values, whether man be conscious or not of the play of the planets upon his psychic centres.

28. Again, it might *seem* good and sufficient logic to say that the individual who attains to intellectual superiority does so through a persistent cultivation of his mentality. But what endows him with these qualities of persistency while his brother, of perhaps greater brain calibre, remains on the dead level of mediocrity? I'll warrant that in the first instance the Sun, Mercury and Mars are suitably conditioned to produce mental energy, or else other astral relationships impel to an all-absorbing ambition to reach a given point; while in the latter case Saturn could so crystallize the brain functions as to produce a mental sluggard, or the Sun and Mars could be too impotent to beget a desire for power. Either ultimation would be presignified in the respective horoscopes, and the result in each as surely foreshadowed as the birth of the morning presignifies the solar elevation at noon.

29. Another factor which enters into the problem of destiny is the one which concerns the *sphere* of activity. The scion of wealth, though his brain potencies be of an inferior quality, has manifestly better opportunities for intellectual unfoldment than has the child of poverty, though he cannot by any manner of means rise higher in the scale of fortune than nature originally intended he should. A proof of this assertion is the fact of a universal ascendancy of "self-made" persons over those of the proverbial golden spoon, while geniuses invariably spring from the lowly born. In the event of two births in the same locality at the same moment of time—which would be a very rare case indeed—though they be socially as far apart as opposite poles, the rise and fall of the astro-magnetic tide in each will be identical, and such as

to attract to each a success or failure as will accord with the respective environments.

30. Or, on the other hand, let us assume that a number of persons of differing degrees of position in the world, all have operating in their nativities a benefic aspect between the Sun and Uranus, in what way would the influence be apportioned? The representative of nobility, if in line of succession, would attain to titular honors; the politician would receive official preferment; the commercial man would enter into a successful business scheme; the clerk would be promoted in his department; while the ordinary day laborer would secure a better "job," or be confronted with the rare and equally pleasing task of accepting better wages. It will thus be perceived that the stars as favor mongers are wholly impartial, dispensing their patronage only in such manner as is consistent with the capacity to receive; just as the numbers of an oratorio, though falling upon numerous ears alike, will affect each but in a measure as to harmonize with the individual attunement.

31. Drummond says, "Laws are only modes of operation, not themselves operators." Man cannot be greater than the Universe; and he is a law unto himself only in so far as Nature makes of him an invincible necessity through which to equilibrate her divine impulses—a contingent though no less an essential factor in a complex fabric whose fiat is one of mutual dependency.

"My own will come to me," but it will come only in its own good time—not through any assumption of personal privilege on my part, but when my star, in its orderly sequence, completes its rainbow arc of promise. Then, and not until then, will I stand related to impinging forces in a polarity of tuneful insistence.

XI

32. "If an ill happening *must* come to pass, why be advised of it, and thereby undergo the needless anxiety involved in a period of anticipation? Why open the door to calamity before it has sought admittance?" One might with equal reason ask why prepare for winter, although its certain coming is a matter within ordinary ken; or, why practice self-denial in order to meet a note whose date of maturity cannot be stayed? "Had I only known!" is but a sorry wail when evoked by the aftermath of the Inevitable. Nor can it be the better part of valor to draw back in fear and trembling from the contemplation of that which may be vouchsafed through known equations in the problems of Destiny. Wisdom never yet did a hurt, and no fractional part of it was ever accorded man for the purpose of working vexation to his spirit. In regard to this question Ptolemy enunciated the following many centuries ago: "For, in the first place, this fact ought to be kept in view, that events which necessarily and fully happen, whether exciting fear or creating joy, if arriving unforeseen, will either overwhelm the mind with terror or destroy its composure by sudden delight; if, however, such events should have been foreknown, the mind will have been previously prepared for their reception, and will preserve an equable calmness by having been accustomed to contemplate the approaching event as though it were present, so that on its actual arrival it will be sustained with tranquillity and constancy."

33. Many there are who regard the presage of a misfortune as equally to be deprecated as the fulfillment thereof—who are of the opinion that at all times it is imprudent to give warning of impending danger. I confess I cannot view the

matter in this light. Enlightenment is never vouchsafed except for a specific purpose, and all inward illumination con-concerning the arcana of the Higher Law tends inevitably to a foreknowledge of things to come. It thus becomes the mission of the seer, by reason of this nearer propinquity with the Godhead, to interpret to the best of his ability the messages that may be revealed to him, whether they be laden with joy, or fraught with the pangs of a promised sorrow. The divine purposes cannot otherwise be so well subserved. The physician who would attempt to withhold from his patient the true condition when hope has taken wings and flown, is unworthy of his calling; for such crisis having to his knowledge been reached, the prophetic amenities demand that the individual be apprised of it, that henceforth the *mind* may the more properly be administered to. The moral courage at the heart of every being is never too weak to face truth. A mother has said to me, "Now that the blow has fallen, I thank you for having forewarned me of the loss of my child, for in great measure I found myself mentally prepared for the shock." That mother possessed not only the courage of the Spartan, but the wisdom of the philosopher. Bear this in mind, what is to be will be, whether the ultimation be known or not. Ofttimes through preconcerted effort certain crises are seemingly nullified or prevented altogether; but who shall say such contingency was not preordained? It is certain that foreknowledge which acts as the apparent hindrance to a presumed purpose is ever attracted through natural activities of some sort, for without an inward magnet of sufficient potency there could be no commensurate attraction. Nature has a way of perfecting her equations regardless of the units which make up the sums; and it is at all times meet that we understand as nearly as possible what our relationship to the impending processes is to be. As said David, "Instruct me to number my days, that I may apply my heart unto wisdom."

XII

34. In one of these papers reference is made to the planets and zodiacal signs as constituting the alphabet of Nature. That Nature should have a language of her own—not a dialect, not a patois, not a provincial hodge-podge, but a method of communication which has to do only with universals—is as patent to the ear attuned to her rhythms as are the passion throbs to the divinity of the poet, or as was the music of the spheres to the soul of the great Kepler.

35. Much of our system of thought, as well as many of our terms of expression, are unconsciously interwoven with the language of the stars. This is a statement that may be easily verified by an examination into the etymology and the basic significance of many words in everyday use, and from which fact one may well infer that the Father of Tongues sits somewhere enthroned in the celestial fabric which envelops and energizes all of animate nature.

36. And to go deeper into the reason for these lingual analogies, one might explain that, as a derivative chord in music is the outcome of a fundamental harmony, so may spoken language be regarded as the reflex of ideas which are generated through planetary impact upon the thought realm. As is well known to the astrologer, Mars begets aggressive tendencies that are bound to be expressed in energetic action or in a fiery verbiage; Saturn induces to a soberness that must find its outlet in close application to a quiet task, or in moanings of despair or discontent. Therefore, in the foregoing sense it is but natural, that words descriptive of certain celestial impulses should be of a character with that planet to which such effect stands the most intimately related.

Let us examine into a few of these words and see if we

haven't all been indulging more or less in Astrology these many, many years, though unwarily to our understanding. The realization might not be pleasant to such as would rather be caught stealing a purse than to run counter with an ingrained, healthy prejudice; but fact, as well as truth, is no respecter of persons, and this is not an age in which honest investigation can be consistently shirked.

37. Now take up your current newspaper, and after the casual survey of its columns you will, perforce, be made to read the headlines of, for instance, a direful railroad *disaster*, the account of which is skillfully wrought by some penny-a-liner whose dome of thought lifts him above all reference to evil stars. Webster defines the word "disaster" as purely of astrological origin, from *dis*, to separate, and *aster*, a star, meaning a malign influence which has emanated or separated itself, from some particular planet. In such an instance as this, while the authorities are diligently probing into a defective signal system in order to arrive at a solution of the occurrence that should have happened a hundred times before had mechanical error been the producer of it, the astrologer will calmly point out to you in his mundane chart the specific cause of the casualty; a casualty which had strangely delayed, in spite of the faulty system referred to, until this particular cause had moved into a position suitable to the astral amenities. And if the victim of this accident receive a cut on the countenance he is told the cut *mars* the same.

38. Sublime truths are often stumbled upon unawares, or practically forced upon one's notice regardless of his seeking. A friend of mine who had for some time good-naturedly pooh-poohed my constancy to so silly a pursuit as Astrology, one day declared that he supposed natures were differently constituted, and that his was of too *jovial* a trend for serious subjects. Asked why he had used that particular adjective, he said he thought it quite well expressed a temperament which

was too jolly, magnanimous and good-natured for abstract nonsense. I forthwith invited him to open my Webster, and he read, "*Jovial*, under the influence of Jupiter, the planet." His face lengthened somewhat, and a thoughtful expression crept into his eyes. Determined to give him no chance to relax yet awhile, I seized a treatise on the subject of Astrology, and opening it at the proper place, bade him run his eyes over the following: "Jupiter strong in a nativity makes a person magnanimous, generous, fond of learning, of a jovial mind, a lover of horses and of outdoor sports" (my friend was a great fancier of horseflesh and went in for polo). What could he say? Like a true Jupiterian, magnanimous in defeat and typical to the last, he gave vent to a hearty "By Jove!" and is to-day a student of Astrology, becoming more and more convinced of its truth as his familiarity with the subject increases.

In that one word he had impulsively given expression to the nature within him, and voiced a language of which one idiom had impressed itself, independently of his volition, upon the thought to be expressed.

39. And likewise is this nature constantly and forever, in symbol and otherwise, manifesting itself around and about us; and man, whether of free choice or not, perpetually responds to the astral vibrations which roll in varying volumes into his psychic sea from out the ocean of the great First Cause. If Venus be the impinging force he is merry or hilarious, loving or sensual, modest or a prude, according to the angle of the refracting element; if Saturn, he is calm or self-centered, a merely frugal person or a miser, reserved or physically timid, all depending upon the dignity of this planet at the time of his nativity. The steadfast worker in quiet lines, the monk, the miser, the organizer who concentrates interests to a given point, are all his children, and characterized in our practical nomenclature as *saturnine* in disposition and tempera-

ment. Diseases which linger, preying upon the flesh and the spirits, belong to his reign, and because of their long-drawn-out endurance the ancients rightfully ascribed them to Chronos, the Greek name for Saturn, and hence comes the word *chronic*, having to do with time; *chronology* belongs to the same parent stem.

40. The Saturn characteristics are directly opposed to those of Mars, just as the Saturn native is antithetic in temperament to the Mars individual. While the one inclines to conservatism and to devotional pursuits, the other revels in conflict and strife, and conducts his enterprises along aggressive lines. Therefore his audacity, energy and self-confidence are fittingly summed up in the term *martial*, which aptly describes the Mars principle as interpreted by Astrology; and though no conscious knowledge be had of its true import, it is nevertheless a word belonging essentially to Nature's vocabulary.

41. In the medical science particularly are to be found glowing instances of Nature speaking through the stars. Of such is the word "chronic" above alluded to, applied to ailments of a contractile, wasting, or of a purulent character, as rheumatism, consumptions, cancerous growths and the like, all of which belong to the Saturn activities. "Venereal distempers" is a term borrowed from the planet Venus, who rules over the reins and loins, the matrix, and members of generation, and to be found so indicated in any textbook on Astrology; and hence the reason why provocatives acting upon the generative system are called "aphrodisiacs," from Aphrodite, the Greek name for Venus. How few of the medical fraternity are aware of the basic truth herein involved. One would suppose these scattering terms so constantly in use by the therapeut, and so pregnant with hints of a divine relationship in the universe, must needs, sooner or later, direct his attention to the open sesame that alone is capable to unravel the many mysteries which enshroud him with a "confusion worse confounded."

Dr. Parker, F.R.S., states that "influenza" was so named in Italy in the seventeenth century "because it was attributed to the 'influence' of the stars." Also, the word "panic" is from the Greek *panikos*, belonging to Pan, who assisted the Athenians at Marathon by creating terrors in the mountain fastnesses to the confusion of the Persians. Pan is Bacchus, otherwise the Sun in Capricorn, to which sign is accorded rule over parts of Persia. Our language is also illumined by the essentially astrological word "pecuniary," as related to Taurus (the Bull), the second sign of the normal zodiac, and is from the Latin *pecunia*, money, and originally came from *pecus*, cattle, signifying property in cattle; and the second house of the horoscope rules over money and cattle.

42. Many examples might thus be adduced wherein Astrology enunciates her truths in words strangely apposite to the principles involved, appearing in different ages and impressing upon various vernaculars the fact of a celestial sovereignty under which all are kindred subjects and to which all must bow alike.

Man-made law is arbitrary, adapting itself to the ever-changing conditions of the social fabric of which he is a part. But the jurisprudence of Nature reposes in the eternal verities, where truth, as revealed by the stellar doctrine, is the same now as it was at the geniture of the world, and as it will be a thousand years hence; and one of these days a fearsome suspicion of this fact will percolate through the cranium of the doubter, and he will wonder if, after all, there isn't "something in it."

XIII

"Man is the quintessence of all the elements, and a son of the universe or a copy in miniature of its soul, and everything that exists or takes place in the universe, exists and may take place in the constitution of man. The congeries of forces and essences making up the constitution of what we call *man* is the same as the congeries of forces and powers that on an infinitely larger scale is called the Universe, and everything in the Universe reflects itself in man, and may come to his consciousness; and this circumstance enables a man to know himself, to know the Universe, and to perceive not only that which exists invisibly in the Universe, but to foresee and prophesy future events."—*Franz Hartmann*.

43. The foregoing reference by Dr. Hartmann to the mutuality of principle involves such an old truth, and one so easy to verify through rightful observation, that the marvel is not so much of its simplicity as to the fact that it is not more generally credited. And yet to the student of Astrology as to no one else there is afforded a justification for those incommensurables in the human temperament which range all the way from clear, spiritual discernment in the one to a non-perceptive state in the other; for he perceives in the respective horoscopes the capabilities and the limitations which are accorded to each as a birthright. He knows that as man unfolds best along the lines of least resistance, the question of soul discernment depends upon adjustment rather than individual mental capacity.

44. Few minds are so constituted as to approach a complex subject without preconceptive hindrances. But in a question of preference commend me to the one whose sentiments are speculative, and therefore open to conviction, rather than to that mind which seeks to discredit a fact simply because it threatens to disturb a conventional habit of thought. While the one is constructive, and in the direction of discovery and growth, the other tends to a subversion of truth, and is a clog in the machinery of progress.

And thus it is there are many things which conspire to retard the advancement of astrological truth: bigotry, preconceived notion, a disinclination to upset grounded opinions, the difficulty of adapting oneself mentally to strange conceptions, and, above all, the incapacity to perceive cognate relationships in the interaction of nature's forces.

45. In this latter respect, and because of its scope, Astrology is perhaps the most useful as well as fascinating of all the sciences; for it not only comprehends the astral and the physical as a duality, but likewise brings under practical survey this fact of a mutual impingement in the subtle laws which constitute the higher and the lower. It teaches the manifest impossibility of estimating natural values except through their relativity with either conjunctive or opposing elements. Nor may one rightly apprehend the why and the wherefore of human predispositions except through their homogeneity with the causative impulses which throb incessantly throughout the Divine Economy.

46. For instance, the sophist would doubtless explain the multiplicity of amours which attend the callings of the actor, the artist, and the musician, as the result of romance, sycophancy, or the emotional weakness in certain natures; never dreaming that the affections, as well as all art, are allied to the Venus activities, and that the very dominancy of this element in the astral organism inclines alike to idealistic channels and to sex attachment. As steel is attracted to the magnet by reason of the Mars sympathy in each, so does the individual whose preponderance of Venus impels him to espouse a Venus calling likewise attract to himself the Venus or love element in surrounding nature.

47. Dr. Pearce, in his "Text-Book of Astrology," vol. ii. 294, writes:

"The *Lancet* once remarked on the singular fact that engineers have, comparatively, an excessive amount of iron in their blood, and attributed this to their absorption of fine particles of iron in the exercise of their calling; the medical writer being, of course, unaware that those who naturally take to engineering are Mars-men, and have, therefore, from birth a large amount of iron and of red corpuscles in their blood. If the engineers as a body were alone distinguished for the redundancy of iron in their blood, it might be attributable solely to their absorption of iron in their occupation, as the *Lancet* surmised; but the same observation holds good with regard to the great majority of surgeons and soldiers, who are martialists and distinguished alike for their energy, pluck, and endurance."

48. The lay mind may readily perceive the force of the logic here involved, without recourse to technical explanation. It need only be added that all observation along these lines must ever tend to the conclusion that Nature operates entirely upon a system of interactions, and comprises in her arcana that fact of a universality of principle such as is touched upon in the above illustrations. And not until Astrology is accorded her parental right as the key to all science, will the investigator be able to unlock the door to the inner chamber, and find Truth.

For Truth is a capricious maid, and while ever seductive in her manner to the modest but persistent suitor who follows closely in her train, she wastes not her witchery upon the mind whose indifference or whose self-sufficiency precludes a proper appreciation of her charms.

XIV

49. "How" and "why" are very insistent factors in the curriculum of life, of a lawful utility when prompted by a genuine desire to know, though ofttimes, I regret to say, they are interposed with an ulterior purpose to confuse an unpopular hypothesis. As for example, the astrologer is frequently challenged to explain just *how* the celestial orbs dispense their unceasing patronage, granting such to be the fact; or *why*, as claimed by the astro-physicist, planets deign to operate upon things sublunary only when in certain relative positions, as a conjunction, sextile, square, etc., and on the other hand to deny their countenance when occupying intermediate positions. Failing of a satisfactory explication of these puzzling propositions, ye captious critic begs to regard the assumption as pure fallacy, and therefore unworthy the consideration of serious minds.

Indeed! Since when did Nature solicit censorship over her divine ordinances? Just when was finite man granted the playful privilege of planting periods along the phraseographs of Infinite law?

50. Whether one would have it so or otherwise, a fact is no less a fact because the "why" and the "how" of it abides somewhere beyond the pale of human perception. The infinitely numerous parts which go to make up the mechanism of a universe revolve and interact through primal modes of adaption, of affinity and proportion, as in gravitation, cohesion, chemical attraction, and such like forces, and will so maintain their relationships with each other despite what one may or may not believe concerning them.

51. Bodies propelled into space would still persist in the thriving habit of returning to earth, whether Newton had dis-

covered the secret of gravitation or not; whether Harvey had or had not come upon the scene, the lifeblood of the animal would continue to course through its proper channels, e'en though all the colleges of physicians throughout time were still to dogmatize upon the rationality (?) of arteries as ducts for the circulation of air. The tides are not going to cease their response to the motions of the Moon just because no logical explanation for the mutual sympathy is forthcoming, or because the supercilious sciolist cannot apprehend *why* they should pay their allegiance to the lesser luminary rather than to the Dog Star, or *why* they should not ebb and flow at any old time.

52. Were truth confined to the limits of demonstrable physics I fear me much of that commodity would be minus a standard of value in the realm of fact. But Nature's law ceases at the behest of no man, and obstinacy, dogmatism, or self-sufficiency as hindrances to understanding, cannot prevent her from indulging in suggestive hints, in striking analogies, and insinuative details that point the way of her doing as surely as the needle indicates the pole. And the operative principles that concentre in and are diffused from out the planetary orbs will continue to conform to their celestial geometry, whether puny man deigns to acknowledge their ubiquitous rule or not.

53. Thousands of years of observation by students spiritually enlightened as regards these arcana, have helped to establish the fact of particular effects attending upon these relationships between interdepending agencies in the celestial organism. The why and the wherefore of these strangely insistent conformities may seem obscure to the unmindful, but, as wrote Lord Bacon, "We are not to deny the existence of a cause in favor of which we have a unanimous agreement of strong analogies, though it may not be apparent how such a cause can produce the effect."

Through analogy is to be found many startling revelations of God's truth working well within the limits of fundamentals sublimely simple, yet how complex as regards the multifold differentiations! A modern philosopher, in line with the Hermetic apothegm as to the identity of the higher with the lower, tells us that "All things in their basic principles resemble all other things, and we are safe in judging of the unknown by the known, of the visible by the invisible, and of the whole by a part."

While as a system of logic analogy may leave one at about the same place he began, it nevertheless affords a serviceable glimpse into the method of natural processes, and the skeptic as regards Astrology need only direct his cynical attention to some of the laws here briefly touched upon to be furnished food for many a long day's reflection. In the meantime let us suggest that no individual has the right to assume an officious attitude toward a subject whose postulates he has not examined, of whose self-eloquent facts he is uninformed, and whose inferences must ever appear to him as irrational quantities by reason of the peculiar trend of his temperament. Astrology has ever been a bugbear to the conventional scientist, owing to its intangibility as viewed from his point of vision, and because the metaphysical and the abstract must necessarily elude materialistic methods of thought and investigation.

54. As expressed by Franz Hartmann, "The greatest difficulty in the understanding of occult laws arises from the circumstance that we cannot perceive remote causes, or seek to connect them with ultimate effects, without being able to see through the intricate network of intermediary causes between the two ends." The how and the why are thus so veiled to the sense perception, and the results to be deduced apparently so far removed from their efficient causes, that concrete logic cannot hope to grapple successfully with the problem. Facts

when not accessible through known principles of argumentation may nevertheless be determined through a rightful observance of coincidences in natural phenomena, of analogies between operative planes of being, and in such like ways as must inevitably force a conviction of the truth of that law of interaction in which reposes the doctrine of the stars.

Granting the wisdom of investigation rather than the indifference which delights in denial, let us see if an earnest enquiry won't disclose a few affirmatory hypotheses more wonderful than are dreamed of in ordinary philosophy.

55. First, be it known that the law of Unity insists upon polarization to a common centre. While a central point of attraction inheres in the atom, the atom as an organized form of energy pays homage to a like principle at the centre of the molecule; and so on gradationally from the lower to the higher, the weaker to the stronger body of potencies, up to the centre of the Universal Structure itself, which maintains its oneness through the comprehensive law of gravity.

56. So, taking Centre as the fundamental premise whence springs every value in Nature's organon, we immediately and with ease perceive its logical correlate, which is Circumference. These are the two propositions of Nature's first syllogism, of which the conclusion belongs more exclusively to the domain of effect. And between Centre and Circumference is the playground of the essences and the integrants whose orderly and incessant motions give meaning to the terms continuity, universality, infinity—comprehended all within the confines of that Circumference in whose very nature is first revealed the principle of the Circle as the manifest form of radiant energy.

Centre is ubiquitous, and yet nowhere, except as a hypothetical point; circumference is an unmeasurable quantity, because it is the embodiment of all that pertains to substance, and for which reason it belongs to the everywhere.

57. Therefore: Assuming a pivotal point as the centre of Unity, and its activity as being necessarily in the nature of expansion, it becomes entirely logical to predicate circular motion as the indispensable prerequisite to every actualizing process, and this through the incessant, cohesive tendency of the smaller to align itself with the greater, and through and by which stability becomes movement, force energy, and unity diversity. Hence, *all is motion*, whether it be vibratory, undulatory, or whatever the theory involved.

In thus establishing our starting point, it should not be difficult to conceive of vibration as the essential modus of motion. All chemico-physical investigation into the atomic world but tends to confirm the truth of an ever-varying change in the molecular energies. This condition of perpetual unrest amongst the ultimate particles is one of Divine necessity, for progress, to be eternal, demands that the principle of movement be extended in all directions to terms of infinity. Were a single atom to hesitate in its orderly function a confusion fatal to the verities would instantly ensue, and everlasting chaos would be writ across the scroll of Time.

58. But creative force, being universal and all-dominant, precludes any such possibility; and whether it be involutional, as in the differentiation of form, or evolutional, as in the centralization of species—utility and adaptation must alike affect the outpouring as well as the upbuilding. Of necessity the sequences along either of these lines are identical, be the ratios of manifestation inverse or reverse, infolding or unfolding: each is dependent upon the same law of harmony—the attraction of like unto like—and without which dictum there could be no distinctive expression in nature.

Hence, conceding active intelligence to the causative or life principle in its act of individualization, the vibratory centres thus set up *must* attract from somewhere out of the primordial essences a responsive movement, else there could be no organization of energy. And energy presupposes Force, which in reality is the causal principle, and in natural phenomena this is ever observed as operating through a system of geometrical ratios in every condition of the universal substance, and to be found variously differentiated according to the angle of impact. *The angle may therefore be considered as the key to the science of harmony, hence the potential factor in all manifestation.*

59. Take the transit of a planet over its nodal points, or where its orbit intersects the plane of the ecliptic, and great disturbances in our magnetic atmosphere will be observed to take place; likewise in music, at the nodes or fixed points of a sonorous chord a change occurs in the vibrations, and harmonic sounds are the result.

Again, a proportion of two volumes of hydrogen to one of oxygen form water; but let the angle of destiny be disturbed or superseded by an excess of either, and to that extent they will remain uncombined. Can any explain why Nature thus hesitates so abruptly at this seemingly slight infraction of a law of proportion? Now, subject this water to a temperature of 60°, and crystallization ensues. But why doesn't the same phenomenon occur at 58° or at 62°? Examine the crystal structures thus formed, and most of them will be found hexagonal in shape, or possessing six projections arranged 60° apart! This may be termed the angle of cohesion, a perfect affinity between the positive and the negative forces in nature. And that is just why *form* has resulted from the union. In other words, this is a combination of the male and female principles, indicated in Astrology by a six-pointed asterisk as the symbol of the *sex*tile aspect.

This unfortunate, proscribed derelict on the scientific sea, Astrology, with the temerity to cry aloud so mystical and fundamental a truth, certainly cannot be impeached because of any haphazard or arbitrary assumption in this particular instance, where *love* is revealed even in the icicle!

And the significance of the 60° aspect may be further exampled by a simple fact in optics, and from which we perceive in the astrological principle a correspondence with the polarization of light; just as phenomena have an analogous bearing on all planes, each to the other respectively. Thus, by reflecting a beam of light at an angle of 56° (a sextile orb) from a clear pane of glass, and receiving it at the same angle of incidence upon a second or similar plane, a ready reflection will be observed when the two planes are parallel to each other, but not so when in perpendicular relationship. As above, the light acquires new properties through polarization. And this aspect in Astrology is essentially of the same import.

60. To understand more clearly the true rationale of angular distances, or "aspects," let us first take the circle of motion as the basic law of manifestation, for in its analysis is to be gleaned the inner significance attaching to the orbits of the celestial bodies, and the inward meaning of their axial and periodical revolutions. As the physical is but the reflection of the spiritual, to the latter must be accorded a geometry identical with that of speculative mathematics, and thus the action of the psychic law in its relation to circles becomes obvious. Accordingly we are led into the metaphysical domains of this geometry, where it is necessary to recognize the analogies between the elements of the circle and the various changes of polarity in the life forces as induced by astral influx; a statement whose real import may be more easily apprehended by the comparison of consecutive points in the daily rotation of the earth upon its axis with certain aspects formed in the circle of the zodiac, the latter comprising twelve signs of which two hours approximately are required for the rising of each. In this wise not only is the corrobora-

Astrosophic Principles

tive emphasis given to the true meaning of the sextile in stellar physics, but additional light afforded upon other and cognate values in the circle of motion.

61. Thus, starting with a given point in the zodiacal circle simultaneously with the moment of sunrise (see chart), we reach the first aspect of importance at 60°, or the sextile (✶), which, as we see, is represented by intersecting lines from the foci of the six-rayed star, or the alchemical symbol for fire

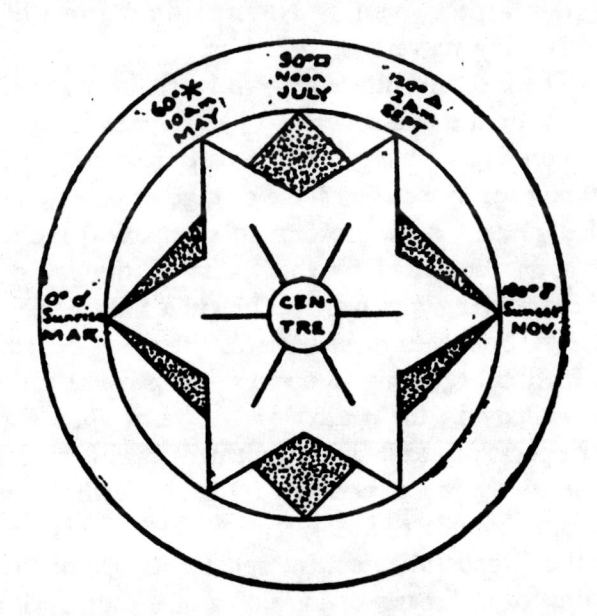

(△) interlaced with that for water (▽). Herein is contained the mystery or sex (sextile, *sextilius*, from *sex*, six), the union of forces, duality, male-female, positive-negative. An equilibrium of forces is thus shown by a combination of heat and moisture, coinciding in the daily circle with the fourth hour after sunrise, when the actinic and luminous principles of the solar ray are the most suitably apportioned to Nature's requirements. By correspondence, similar qualities not only belong to this 60° point from the major syzygy, but to every arc of the same measurement. In the year circle, commencing with the Sun's entry into Aries, this aspect accords with the May period, when the proximate principles of vegetation are most actively in process. As truly expressed by Addison—"The spring bears the same figure among the seasons of the year that the morning does among the divisions of the day, or youth among the stages of life." If the sage needed any vindication of his claim as regards the essential character of this aspect, here is Nature's incontrovertible testimony proclaiming its verity.

The next definite point we reach in our circle is the 90° aspect, or the evil square (□). Dynamically this is correct as representing a right angle to our starting point, an angle of violence by reason of the change in potentiality which here takes place. As a problem in mechanical philosophy it may be aptly illustrated by that point in the arc of a projectile where, having attained the height of its velocity, a moment of rest, or rather displacement, ensues preparatory to its law of motion beginning to operate in a reverse ratio. This finds its analogy in the season of the year when Nature reverses her operations and the sap element begins to coagulate; likewise to the noon period of the day, when the element of moisture yields to the reign of heat. This angle or square in the Hippocratic doctrine represents one of the crises in the course of a disease, because of a quadrature with the zodiacal point of seizure. It is here made patent that the truth involved is something much more recondite than mere phantasy or empirical assumption.

This point being passed, an acceleration takes place, as with the projectile—though in the human economy it is more in respect of psychic gravity—and we reach the next aspect, 120°, that of the trine (△), symbol of fire. The heat or life forces are now augmented, coinciding with the second hour after noon in the daily circle, and with the fruitage season of the solar revolution. Its character as an angle of attainment, and the "why," is thus as obvious as is the mid-afternoon Sun.

The next magneto-spiritual point is the opposition (☍), 180°, the half of the circle of motion, the sunset of the day, and the period of negation in the life forces of the year. Its symbol is aptly depicted, showing a counterposed spiritual activity. The symbol itself is a combination of the alchemical glyphs for day (☉) and night (☽), the positive and the negative in juxtaposition. In truth, the symbol for the astrological conjunction (☌) should be reversed when used in association with a feminine or negative planet. The conjunction itself, with its circle and projecting line, typifies the extension of some specific influence; or, more clearly illustrated, a faster moving planet, having passed the body of a slower moving one, carries forward or extends to another point the vibratory essences of the one passed.

62. The doctrine of "aspects" is thus seen to possess not only a mathematical, but a chemic and metaphysical relevancy, and indeed involves a proto-chemistry of a significance in comparison with which other branches of physics can trace only the externals of the microcosmic unit. For through these are determined the mutual gravities that unite one sidereal element with that of another, translated into dispositional and constitutional meanings—the issues and percentages of which are duly proportioned according to the type and measure of the angle and the respective dignities or debilities of the combining factors. And this applies as well to corresponding mixtures of cognate elements or substances belonging to all kingdoms of evolutionary life, whether of form, of color, of sound, or whatever the organization.

63. That vibration or motional impulse—be it etheric, magnetic, dynamic, or what-not—is itself the substance or expression of that mysterious thing called Life, may be

accepted as axiomatic. But the further proposition that this life-energy under no circumstance ever registers itself in what is termed a straight line, may not so readily yield assent. Why? Such would involve abrupt terminals known as beginning and end—supposititious quantities of no mathematical value in a law of Infinitude. That which is geometrically and for relative purposes called a *line* starts with a point or sphere, and the intervening space between any two such centres of energy is but a succession of concentric spheres or circuits of action. So from the near-ultimate atom, through the manifold realms of individualized potencies, up to the ponderous planet that revolves about its solar centre—all are but wheels within wheels, integral multiples of the primal Unity, therefore expressions of the one distinct and fundamental principle that inheres in the centre of every circle or cycle; and in a universe of ceaseless activity the processes of unfoldment—which are reiterative just as number as an expression of unity is necessarily multiplicative—cannot otherwise than operate through a code of spherical influences.

64. Hence the doctrine of the sphere, whereby one is enabled to perceive and to interpret the relations that co-exist between definite angles created by the intersection of one circle with another. And these angles are but measurements of vibration—spheres of vibrant consciousness—whose values are determined by the boundaries of the particular segment of the circle of their field of operation, and the modus and rationality of which are quite as discernible—and more than theoretically corroborative—in the atomic as in the stellar worlds. Thus, it has been demonstrated that the soul-strains induced by the violin bow travel along the vibratory ethers and polarize themselves into determinate figures most suggestive of those involved in astral physics, as shown by the following excerpt from an article in the *Arena* a few years ago:

"Lichtenberg's electric figures suggested to Chladni the notion of discovering the state of vibration of plates, excited by the bow of a violin, acting on sand freely scattered on their upper surface. . . . Vibrations are induced by the violin bow drawn against the outer rim. The sand at once arranges itself in radii, falling into the non-vibratory parts of the plate's surface. These angles, though notably limited, are mathematically consistent, and exhibit definite portions of the circle, such as a semi-sextile, sextile, semi-square, or their multiples, as the trine or square. So far as this experiment goes, it appears to suggest that these angles, which are prime factors in an astrological figure, actually inhere in the natural workings of vibratory force in space. It is presumptive that the laws which call them into effect act in response to vibrations in areas of the ether, caused by planetary excitements exerted upon the plane of the ecliptic.

"The results and probable workings of a general natural law are shown by collective instances like these, when the curves and radii produced are of a precise and permanent character, admitting of exact measurement, as here, and it would seem that they furnish the principal present mode of approaching the question of the probable influence on organized life of the vibrations excited by the movements of bodies in space. We have to deal, in our enquiry, with definite periodic phenomena which, with the constant and uniform changes of the vibrations, return time after time to the same value."

65. This law of geometrical necessity may be regarded as a fundamental one in every department of physics. And though the higher in form the nearer is the approach to the circle and the sphere, yet be it known that *the point at which the plane of one circle may intersect that of another is an impinging angle, without which there can be no manifesting relationship between the two.* Herein reposes the doctrine and the rationale of the astrological "aspect." It was observed by Haüy that in crystallization the decrease in the successive layers of integrant molecules took the angle as a point of departure; the seven valencies, or combining powers, in chemistry are analogical with certain vibratory ratios as treated of in the science of acoustics; while spectrum analysis reveals the action of internal forces as manifesting through periodic motion within the molecule.

Now, the same law obtains in the sidereal heavens as in the lesser firmaments of the molecule and the atom; the planets are but the bigger atoms, the mightier centres of energy, describing in their orbital motions the greater circles in the Universal Sphere or *primum mobile*.

66. In Astrology the zodiacal belt is the principal centre of radiation in our system, because it encloses the ecliptic, or path of the Sun, who is our centre of attraction as well as diffusion. Bodies moving along this celestial highway form certain definite angles, termed astrological aspects, which are nothing more nor less than points of contact for, primarily, the induction of solar energy, and, secondarily, a proportional influx of the magnetism of such forces as may thus stand related to each other. And in all "God geometrizes."

And in this wonderful geometry is involved the origin and the circumstance of Man—that interrogative creature who asks to know not only the Whenceward of his coming, but the Witherward and the intricacies of his destiny, that he might the more intelligently direct the purpose and so "rule his stars."

> Paracelsus wrote: "The action of the macrocosmic influence stimulates the corresponding elements existing in man into action . . . because the latter is the son of the astral body of the Macrocosm in the same sense as the physical body of man is a son of the earth" (*Labyrinthus Medicorum*). Again: "There is an attractive power in the soul of man which attracts physical, mental, and moral diseases from the Chaos. The planetary influences extend through all Nature, and man attracts poisonous qualities from the Moon, from the stars, and from other things; but the Moon and the stars and other things also attract evil influences from man, and distribute them again by their rays, because Nature is an undivided whole, whose parts are intimately connected."

This has reference to man in ordinary, not to the evolved ego, and states in general terms the fact of a related sympathy as existing between the Microcosm and the Macrocosm; the co-attraction being only according to the essences and the predispositions of one's own constitution.

The foregoing statement involves a qualifying truth but little pondered, and as rarely apprehended, and it is this: He who becomes regenerate in body and in mind is exempt from sublunary affections, in that he is no longer subject to attraction and absorption of noxious astral fluids; the physical organism purged of its poisons, and the Soul "defecated from the dregs of sense," no longer provide correlates to give lodgment to malevolent entities, planetary or otherwise. This adjustment of the constitutional aberrancies into higher normalities is the alchemy that transmutes the baser metals (animal qualities and passions) into faculties responsive only to the symphonies of the Universe; for such a one vibrates in perfect harmony with the Centre of all life. He has fulfilled the requirements that attend the "remission of sins." And this is the wise man who rules his stars (thoughts, emotions, etc.), and none otherwise.

Unfortunately, here and there is one who loudly acclaims himself such a ruler, though unversed in the ordinances or the experiences of either physical or spiritual alchemy, and so dons the cap of the "wise man"; under, similarly, the same illusion as the one who boasts a putative intimacy with the Cosmic Consciousness while yet a prey to vertiginous whimsies and the stomach ache.

However, one may possess speculative knowledge of a fact, though a non-partaker of the experience and the wisdom which such fact involves; just as one may know the philosophy of diet and hygiene in words and not in works; or have a theoretical apprehension of mystical arcana, but with no legitimate claim to adeptship—be chock-full of theological lore, and yet not know God.

In these connections, and as to one's place on the path, we are constrained to say that the karmic potentials in a natal scheme are something which esoteric Astrology at present but negatively discerns. No absolute distinctions are discoverable between the horoscope of genius and that of mediocre possibilities despite the rules which differentiate between idiocy and talent. The faculty of inspiration as the token of an older soulhood may easily supplant and transcend an exceeding capacity for the intellectual effort that must remain content to *believe* instead of to *know*. The antitheses are doubtless properly registered in the birth figure, and to be clearly perceived if one could but lift a corner of the veil and fathom the sequence of past lives.

I have noted, however, in connection with this problem of regeneration as concerns the inherent capacity to achieve the same, that planets posited in closing degrees of signs may be viewed as evidence of soul ripeness for this mantle of divinity, though the condition must be attended with a commensurate measure of the devotional strain to provide the necessary spiritual afflatus.

This especially as regards the "fixed" signs, in which are respectively housed the four Royal Stars; and of greater significance, the end of Taurus, where abide a group of nebulous stars essentially subjective in their import. Their bearing upon the actinic or germinative activities of the springtime is also suggestive, for the vernal season is presided over by Venus, the ruler of Taurus and the goddess of love or unifying principle in Nature, whose associate in the fecundative processes is Mercury (Hermes, the Initiator), the Divine Water (*Mer*) that laves and impregnates the fecund soil and renders it subject to generation.

And so with the human soul (soil) that attains to the telestic junction with pure spirit; which is effected through the lustral waters of Regeneration—the *salvation* described by Thomas Vaughan, the mediæval mystic, as "nothing else but transmutation." And this is the true and only covenant that entitles one to the claim of mastery of fate, the rulership of one's stars.

Seek to understand the XVIIth Arcane of the Tarot (the Star of the Magi), whose cognate is Mercury and whose signature is the letter Pe of the Hebrew alphabet, and much may be gleaned of the real functions of Mero-pe, that daughter of the Pleiades (at the end of Taurus) who married a mortal.

There is not a point of the Zodiac that does not provide a key to unlock some gate that leads into the adyta of the Mysteries. Similarly do the classic myths contribute illuminative analogues of truths that lie hid in the secret chambers of the astrological organum.

Astrology and Medicine

XV

In the estimation of a very great many, Astrology is concerned chiefly with selfish abettals, blind credulities, chicken culture, lucky hours, planetary hair-tonic, and the like assortment of equations and wonder-marvels. In this visionary view human frailty is of itself severely arraigned on account of the charlatanry that all too frequently dishonors a true doctrine of the stars, for a questionable service must inevitably attend the imprudent demands of *desiderata curiosa*.

And yet, misguided opinion such as this is scarcely censurable, considering that until very recent years the supine interest in the subject, coupled with narrow bigotry in high places, left the fact undisclosed that the very inner arcana of man's whole being were wrapped up in its ordinances, and that in these same ordinances reposed the key to the planal sequences that relate him to every department of the universal consciousness, the key that unlocks those wondrous mysteries of correspondence whereby is revealed the kinship that obtains throughout the various avenues of manifestation.

67. The ancients recognized in Astrology the only absolute key to the Healing Art, because it pointed the way into the very inner chamber of Nature's arcana. Without it the doctrine of signatures would be a very sorry doctrine indeed. With this searchlight of science one may enter any domain he chooses, and yet observe the same wonderful analogies which proclaim the omnipresence of the One Law. Dame Nature is a stickler for form in spite of her varied peregrin-

ations, and though she is wont to assume apparently different garbs her dresses are all fashioned after the same fundamental principle. There may be changes of combination in color and tone, but no essential variance will be found in the basic pattern as first designed by this *modiste par excellence*.

68. In some of her divergences she chooses the blue of Saturn as the primary tone in manifestation, as in lead, or in the element termed *cold;* again she affects the yellow of Venus, and in this diffusive gown she introduces herself into the mineral kingdom as Madame *Copper,* or in the emotional realm as the personification of *Love.* Though anon in *peppery* vein she draws about herself the *red* mantle of Mars, and with fierce purpose and an *iron* will she scatters *energy* where'er she lilts.

69. So, whether moving majestically in the sidereal heavens, on tour through the vegetable, the animal, or the mineral provinces, or playing upon the gamut of human emotions, she reveals herself in seven specific moods as indicated in the order of the planets. To apprehend the import of one of these individual moods on any one plane, is to have divined its full significance throughout the whole of universal nature.

70. As Paracelsus says—"The natural forces acting in the various organs are intimately related to similar forces in the organism of the world; and as the liver, the spleen, the heart, etc., are the bodily representatives of certain activities, likewise the Sun and Moon, Venus, Mars, etc., are visible representatives of the corresponding organs of the Cosmos. If a man get angry it is not because he has too much bile, but because the Mars, the combative element in his body (the invisible power that guides the production of bile), is in a state of exaltation." It was the spiritual cognition of this interdependence of *principle* that constituted Paracelsus the greatest physician the world has known. He read nature in the light of Truth, wherein order and harmony, impulse and response, are de-

pendent attributes, as revealed in these similitudes which co-exist throughout all her kingdoms. "If I have manna in my constitution, I can attract manna from heaven. Melissa is not only in the garden, but also in the air and in heaven. Saturn is not only in the air, but deep in the earth and in the ocean. What is Venus but the artemisia that grows in your garden?"

71. And what is rosemary but the sun?—who has his exaltation in Aries, which rules the head: hence, is a prophylactic against giddiness and swimmings therein, lethargy, etc. *Similia similibus curantur.* The qualities of the Sun being warmth (life), it also cures by antipathy the cold distempers of Saturn, such as coughs, phthisis, consumptions, etc., by conveying heat and dryness to the thin distillations characteristic of those disorders. *Contraria contrarii curantur.* Needless to say that to be properly vitalizing the herb must be gathered and administered according to the operations of its star. It may also be of interest to know why decoctions made from the above plant are so efficacious in the treatment of impaired eyesight, rheums, cataracts, and affections incidental to the eye. The sympathy arises through the Sun's dominion over the eyes and the solar nature of the plant, as will be found explained in any treatise on medical astrology. The metaphysician, guided by his knowledge of the law of correspondences, rightly attributes these disorders to mental emotion, which, in sense action, is allied to the spleen, conceded by all astrologers to be ruled by Saturn (melancholy), the polar opposite of the Sun.

72. From Saturn, the Chronos of the ancients, comes the word *chronic,* explanatory of the attributes of this planet, which affect in a tedious and lingering manner. Thus, Saturn, if suitably conditioned in the celestial organism at the birth of an individual, may induce either to consumption or cancer, which a proper introduction of the Mars or energizing ac-

tivities may neutralize and cure. The modern medico, in his pleasure hunts for gerrymandering germs and baffling bacilli, does not perceive this, for in searching with unseeing eyes he never thinks to inquire as to *their* divine cause, nor realizes that parasitical growth is but *coincident as an effect with the disease itself.*

But the medicine of the apothecary school lost its divinity at about the same period that physical astronomy repudiated its soul. Each is still truanting outside the breastworks, sublimely unconscious of the feast of Truth in progress at the center of the citadel.

73. As aptly stated by Paracelsus—"The star-gazer knows only the external visible heavens; but the astrologer knows two heavens, the external visible one and the internal invisible one. There is not a single invisible power in heaven which does not find its corresponding principle in the inner heaven of man; the Above acts upon the Below, and the latter reacts upon the former." What physician, if he be unacquainted with astral law, can explain why *symphytum* (the Saturn herb *comfrey*) is such an excellent healing expedient in instances of fractured bones? Is he aware of the fact that the bony structure of man is ruled by Saturn, and furthermore that any fomentation applied to the affected part when the Moon is transiting the place of Saturn at the individual's nativity would be very slow and unsatisfactory in its results? Which impels me to quote once more from Paracelsus: "Our physicians pay no attention to the position of the planets, and therefore they kill more patients than they cure, because a medicine that may do good at one time may be injurious at another, according to the prevailing influence. *That which is active in medicines is their astral elements* acting upon the astral man, and they are produced by astral influences, and it makes the greatest difference whether a medicine is pervaded by one influence or another."

Now need one wonder why the present school of medicine, in alienating itself from the astrological principia, goes floundering in the quagmire of Experimentalism? Or, why Dr. Sharp, the noted English physician, should have deplored the fact that "the orthodox system of medicine is still without any law, and is in a condition like that of navigation before the discovery of the mariner's compass."

XVI

74. Astrology is so generally associated with the art of vaticination *pur et simple,* that the casual thinker in his careless contemplation of it has been unheedful of one of its greatest purposes—the scientific exposition of the laws of disease and health.

And yet, when venturing into the realm of Cause in search of a solution to the fundamental problems which affect our being, what more natural than to be led to the unraveling of the skein of destiny itself? Does not the chemist, by virtue of his knowledge of the physical elements and the laws of admixture, predicate the way from simple to compound? Does not the discerning mind, when contemplating the lucid arrangement of a set of orderly premises, jump readily and with foresight to the logical inferences to be deduced?

75. The spirit of prophecy is integral with the human mind, because the human mind is one with that illimitable nature which is constantly evolving series upon series of sequences along the avenues of manifestation from cause to

action, and action to effect. And thus it is but a normal tendency in man, when conversant with a chain of causes, to assume with confidence a presupposition of homogeneal effects.

The rationality of the stellar doctrine in this particular, cannot therefore be questioned, and it is not my purpose here to attempt any justification of its predictive claims, only in so far as those claims relate to the astral nature—or genesis, development, and culmination—of corruptions in the physical organism.

76. Modern medical science, resting upon a putative basis, is not only confessedly ignorant of the origin of disease, but of the curative action of physic as well; therefore amenable to the vagaries of a doubtful pathology. No other condition can be expected so long as it refuses to look beyond the confines of bodily tissues and physical atoms into that world of causative forces whence alone the subsequent processes may be followed and understood. Only recently a prominent physician came forward with the announcement of a discovery that cancer was caused by animal parasites. Innocent protozoa! As well affirm that animal putrefaction is due to the presence of maggots! "Those who merely study and treat *effects* of disease are like persons who imagine that they can drive winter away by brushing the snow from the door. It is not the snow that causes the winter, but the winter is the cause of the snow." (Paracelsus.)

77. Far be it from my purpose to cast any disrespect upon those noble followers of the healing art to whom the amelioration of human suffering is as a religion; and there are many such, but they are physicians by virtue of the nature within them, and despite the empiricism of a defective curriculum.

The medical faculties of to-day are little concerned with the spiritual, or the inner arcana which constitute the divine selfhood of the *real* man, and which is one with the Universe; hence, lack information relative to the very groundwork of his constitution. The astrologer contends, as did the ancient physicians—such as Cardan, Galen, Hippocrates—that in the heavens alone may one hope to find the key to the occult secrets of nature; not in viewing these mighty wanderers as objects merely to be—as Zadkiel puts it—"photometrically and photographically" disported with, but studied as sublime symbols of the Law of Unity which stamps its one and immutable method upon every organized state of being. Such is comprehended in the doctrine of correspondences, and amplified in the tenets of Astrology.

78. The term unity implies a mutual dependence, a mutual likeness, mutual values, between the integral parts of the whole. Therefore one may readily accept the fact that man is not only a universe in miniature, a sidereal organism similitudinary with the greater cosmos, but that he possesses all of its potentialities centralized into specific physiological functions that correspond to the orbs of the planetary system. And as with the heavenly bodies so with these centres in man; they have their times of exaltation or depression according to the expansion or contraction of the inner elements which compose his astral atmosphere. Furthermore, as the Divine Will manipulates the movements of the starry hosts, so does man's will —an emanation of the Divine—govern the operations in his own celestial firmament.

79. These astral centers may be likened to the tympanum of the ear, but whereas that organ is capable only to receive and register physical vibration, the stars of the inner man may respond to and absorb the outside astral essences, and thereby, if such be of a vitiating or antipathetic nature, engender disease, which is but a condition of discord in the astral vibrations, superinduced by impinging forces of a dissimilar character. It will be clearly understood, however, that the susceptibility must be inherent in the physical organism, else no responsive influence from the stellar world will find a lodg-

ment therein. The following example will elucidate this statement: If a man's Sun (heart) at his birth be favorably conciliated with his Saturn (spleen), then these astral principles will be harmoniously related in their physical expression, and any subsequent transit of this planet over his Sun can affect him but little; but if otherwise, the functions of these organs will be greatly disturbed at the period of such phenomena.

Hereby is illustrated that law of sympathy and antipathy which supervenes throughout the universal cosmos, for

> "All are but parts of one stupendous whole,
> Whose body nature is, and God the Soul."

In this idea of unity reposes the truth of intracosmic law, a conversancy with which is essential to the intelligent diagnosis and prognosis of disease.

XVII

80. *Veritas in puteo* was a saying of the ancient sages: "Truth lieth at the bottom of a well." This was but a clever way of asserting that the principle of a thing was inherent with the center, and could not be cognized by superficial scrutiny. No examination of an *effect*, how minute soever, will profit the student who cannot perceive therein the congenital reflex of an essential *cause*. Nor until he apprehend the *principle* of that cause will he be able to deal intelligently with the effect.

81. The empiricism of the modern medicaster is but the natural outgrowth of a persistent refusal to examine into the

law which governs the spiritual activities of the physiological system, or to recognize in the doctrine of correspondences the self-evident fact of an identity between sidereal man and the celestial fabric which revolves about him. Until there is a formal concession made to the stellar hypothesis, the wave of doubt and the current of uncertainty must continue to disturb the surface waters of the well of science, whilst truth remains unperceived in the crystal sands at the bottom.

82. It does not seem that this doctrine of correspondences, as elucidated in Astrology, ought to be considered at all incongruous with natural philosophy. Nature disporteth not with a multitude of methods in the execution of her ordinances. A principle is a principle, whether it repose in the center of an atom, or in the solar point of a sidereal world. The principle of Venus is identical wherever found, be it expressed as love in the human emotions, or as the active basis of copper in the metallic kingdom; as yellow in the color scheme, or as the impelling energy of the reins in the physiological system. And no note is sounded in Nature's register that does not receive responsive vibrations from kindred notes, though anon a discord is aroused in one diametrically opposite in attunement. This latter is *the initial step in the condition termed disease.*

83. Lest the claim that Astrology is the legitimate interpreter of the medical principia be deemed a baseless assumption, or lacking the scientific endorsement which this age demands of a strange doctrine, I call your attention to the following statements by learned philosophers in natural law.

Culpepper, the noted English physician of the seventeenth century, wrote: "Such as study Astrology are the only men I know that are fit to study physic, physic without Astrology being like a lamp without oil."

Aristotle affirmed that "the vital heat and radical moisture were qualities entirely celestial, produced from the light of the sun and moon, with the concurrence of all the other stars." (Placidus.)

Galen, the author of numerous books on medicine, cautioned the people of his time "not to trust themselves to that physician (or rather pretender) who is not skilled in Astrology."

Hippocrates, styled the "father of medicine," asserted that "the man who did not well understand Astrology was rather deserving to be called a fool than a physician."

Paracelsus maintained that "a physician who knows nothing about cosmology will know little about disease."

84. A physician in the London press writes: "I am certain that new moons, and the last remnant of dying moons, have distinct influence. This has often been evidenced to me in my midwifery practice. Why are labor pains strong during a new moon and feeble at the end of a lunation? Why are diseases of an acute or inflammatory character in the first quarter, and more lingering and chronic in the last? Why do medicines act better when the moon is at the full, particularly a solar remedy for a solar disease, e. g., gold in heart disease?"

Here is a man whose observation discloses to him a significant fact that is repeatedly brought to his notice; but were he to propound his theory to a board of non-cogitative medicos to whom the celestial luminaries, and the vital heat and radical moisture referred to by Aristotle, are unknown as homogeneous principles, what, think you, *could* be their reply? So strong is unreasoning prejudice, that it is doubtful if a multitude of facts such as the above, multiplied *ad infinitum*, would induce them to a recognition of the relationship between these cosmic principles and organic nature. And yet in the last point cited by the London practitioner, that of the magnetic action of medicine at full moon, we have but the simple instance of the vital heat (Sun) and the radical moisture (Moon) in celestial nature arriving at a neutral point of expression, whereat cognate influences are more operative in such structures as are related thereto, of which the heart and brain are specific examples, because governed respectively by the sun and moon.

85. From which simple illustration of planetary efficiency one may easily go further, and assume that from out the congeries of celestial forces, "the sun and moon, and the concurrence of all the other stars," there must emanate manifold causes which produce diverse effects in the organic world, according to the commixion of the influences involved. An unbiased examination of such facts as are constantly passing unobserved, could not otherwise than lead to the ultimate conviction that the ancients "knew a thing or two" which it were well for the modern Æsculapians to render heed to.

86. "Without a compass," wrote Dr. Sharp; and it was Baron Liebig who said, "Truly one is tempted to adopt the opinion, that among the sciences which have for their object a knowledge of nature and her forces, medicine as an inductive science occupies the lowest place."

This statement by so eminent an authority in medical jurisprudence should afford food for reflection. It also involves a problem, the solution to which lies in *recovery*, not *discovery*.

XVIII

87. Considered by astrological standards there is no class of individuals so adapted by temperament to scientific research, to experimental analysis, to occult dialectics, and therefore to genuine discovery, as is the medical fraternity. This is because they function principally under Scorpio, whose ac-

tivities endow with keenness of discernment, fertility of imagination, and resource in adaptation. This division of the Zodiac is oft referred to in Astrology as the "medical sign," combining as it does in its natives the innate magnetic, curative faculty with incisiveness of judgment, and skillfulness in handicraft.

88. There is a higher and a lower functional plane in each of the zodiacal domains, but in none are these so widely divergent, or so palpable in the expressive side of their nature as in that of Scorpio, because this sign is essentially forceful and self-assertive. It therefore becomes either one of the strongest, or else one of the weakest signs of the twelve, according as the higher or the lower predominates.

89. The spiritual Scorpio is intense and concentrative in its efforts to uplift humanity, to ameliorate human suffering, and to effect a universal betterment in the body politic. Such is the palliative or constructive side in its expression. The materialistic Scorpio is sensual, tricky, crafty, money-getting, and indifferent to affliction if only extra dollars and cents may be made to multiply in the forced quickening of a patient's pulse-beat. This is its destructive side, or the function of Dissolution as portrayed by the sign.

90. Naturally both planes of the Scorpio qualities are to be found represented in the ranks of the medicaster: the humanitarian, the searcher after Truth with a capital T, the truly great; and on the other hand many, many whose sole object is to emulate the offices of the leech which are too often resorted to, and who refuse to countenance any fact not incorporated in a recognized text-book. Needless to say, the Hippocrates', the Paracelsus', the Harveys and the Hahnemanns are not of this latter.

91. But doubtless these opposite expressions to be found in all departments of Nature are indispensable to her higher plan, for only through relation is truth to be discerned. There would be no use for a lever if there were not a fulcrum, no

criterion if not an avenue of comparison, no standard of judgment if not an adverse phase to give it plausibility.

92. This line or reasoning, when applied to the methods of the two schools of medicine, must demonstrate the necessity of each in its proper place, for this fact of duality in all natural processes is as patent here as elsewhere. But as spiritual physics teaches us that there can be no duality without a trinity, and dynamics proves that all motion which comprehends a north and south pole, as in spherical bodies, must take account of an equatorial line, so in all logic there is to be found a true and essential line of equilibration between any two diametrically opposite theories; while either of which if emphasized alone would mean the detriment of each.

I maintain that this balancing power, this third element which constitutes the triad in all philosophy and in all science, and in medicine particularly, is comprehended in the astrological principia, the art which harmonizes the two, and through cognizance of which only may order come out of chaos.

93. Thus, while one school espouses the law of sympathy the other advocates the theory of dissimilars. Both are right, and yet both are wrong, paradoxical as the statement may appear, for there is but a half truth in each. It is a poor rule that won't work both ways, and as stated by Culpepper, "Sympathy and antipathy are two hinges upon which the whole model of physics turns; and that physician who minds them not is like a door from off the hooks, more like to do a man mischief than to cure him."

94. But properly to appreciate this double doctrine, a knowledge of astral law is a desideratum. For instance, if a patient be suffering from a Mars, or febrile disorder, and that planet is afflicted from a sign in which he holds dignity, i. e., of a nature allied to his activities, then a martial remedy would be the true corrective, for in this case harmony could even-

Astrosophic Principles

tuate only through *sympathy*. But should Mars as the prime mover be in a sign through which he can exert no healthy attraction, then the medicines of Venus—who is his polar opposite—would need be resorted to, and restoration would result through *antipathy*. Or, as Paracelsus illustrates: "In a case of dropsy (ruled by the Moon), it would be exceedingly dangerous to give any remedy that would help to attract the evil influences of the moon; but the sun is opposed to the moon, and those remedies which attract the astral essences of the sun will counteract those of the moon, and thereby the *cause* of dropsy may be cured."

95. Practicing medicos often find themselves perplexed to know why a certain line of treatment avails in one instance and meets with failure in another—is operative for good at one time, and either harmful or barren of results at another. That such are pathological facts in practical medicine cannot be denied, and yet with the mystic key at hand, where it has lain for centuries rusty from disuse, it remains for some one, free of scientific disdain and self-sufficiency, to utilize it for its ordained purposes.

96. It is indeed a sad reflection upon the spirit of the times, that the divine science of Astrology should lie neglected and dust-begrimed on the highway to Knowledge, praying for a chance inspection by the unseeing eyes which contemptuously pass it by. But, alas, the mere suggestion of astral physics as of essential utility in the science of therapeutics is almost enough to throw a body of unsuspecting medicos into a panic; and to beard the medical lion in its den with such a declaration would be to risk incarceration for *lunacy;* though perhaps after due thought there might be some hesitation in applying to the malady a name so insinuative of Dame Luna, who wields particular sway over the department of the brain.

97. Apropos of this reference to mental affections, I might cite another instance of the astral theory in the treatment

of disease. Insanity being due to a disorganization of the lunar activities, may be counteracted by a solar remedy, for the same reason as mentioned above for dropsy. Paracelsus demonstrated this fact by the successful use of St. Johnswort (*Hypericum perforatum*), alchemically prepared, in cases of obsession, epilepsy and madness; in fact, he states that "hypericum is almost a universal medicine," doubtless because of the solar sympathy inherent with it. The Sun, as asserted by Aristotle, and so recognized in Astrology, governs the vital energy.

98. The statement has been made in these papers that a knowledge of intracosmic law is necessary to the correct diagnosis of disease; in which connection I beg the reader's forbearance while I relate a personal incident which occurred in my professional work some years ago. A gentleman, an utter stranger and in great stress of mind, called to ask if Astrology could tell him the nature and outcome of his mother's ailment. He was unable to give her birth data, so casting a figure for the time of the query I stated as my judgment that the lady was hopelessly afflicted with cancer. He then gave the information that this was exactly the question at issue with the three physicians who had held a consultation that morning, one maintaining it was cancer, the other two stoutly protesting against the idea. Suffice it to add, that the lady succumbed to the ravages of cancer in less than six months from the time of consultation. And thus Astrology, in the absence of the patient, furnished a correct diagnosis whereon a clinic of physicians, with the advantage of personal examination, had failed to agree. And yet the writer disclaims any familiarity with the theory or practice of medicine, though he does confess to a slight acquaintanceship with some of the fundamentals as expounded by Astrology, which proclaims the fact of a unity and an orderly impingement of forces that vibrate systematically throughout the domain of nature.

And these are truths which a child might perceive, except he persist in keeping the windows of his soul tightly closed, that the eyes of his intellect might see "as in a glass, darkly."

XIX

99. The recently well-authenticated cure of a case of cancer of the throat by the application of violet leaves to the affected part, occasioned not a little surprise as well as serious discussion in medical circles. This diagnosis, concurred in by several prominent specialists, was further confirmed by the Chemical Research Association after a careful analysis of portions of the growth, thereby settling all questions as to its cancerous nature.

100. Despite the professional interest thus attaching to the case, the real importance of the treatment—and the most far-reaching if only viewed in the light here suggested—is vested in the astrological claim that all plant life, zodiacally considered, is sympathetically related to respective parts of the human organism. The pertinency in this instance rests in the fact that the violet is ruled by Venus, whose domal dignity is Taurus, the *throat* sign, and not in the probability of its being a universal mitigant in all cancerous growth, wheresoever located. Were the intestinal tract (Virgo) the seat of attack, it is unlikely a violet poultice would prove of unusual efficiency.

101. And it is just here that physicians, unmindful of the interaction of astral law, so often get sidetracked in experi-

mental therapeutics. They are ofttimes sorely puzzled after the successful action of a newly discovered agent, to find it so surprisingly *nil* in the next instance, and naturally are prone to accredit the subsequent failure to an erroneous deduction in the initial case; whereas in reality two separate and distinct natures, though seemingly identical, have been treated. It is not a part of their present ethics to know that a medicine whose specific value accords with the Taurus sphere in the organic world may not exert so protean a virtue as that of stimulating, for instance, the Capricorn or the Pisces activities, though it might prove a successful remedy in the Scorpio realm through the law of antipathy, providing the afflicting planet be out of its dignities.

102. By reason of this Venus sympathy, the leaves and flowers of the violet are equally efficacious in all ailments of the throat, as tonsilitis, diphtheria, quinsy, etc., though these disorders, being inflammatory, partake of the Mars nature, whereas cancer is Saturnine because commencing with induration (a *crystallisation* of the glands) and developing into phadenic conditions of chronic (*Chronos,* Saturn) malignancy.

That there is nothing new in this treatment, note what Culpepper wrote in the seventeenth century: "Violet is a pleasing plant of Venus . . . used to cool any heat or distemperature of the body . . . to drink the decoction of the leaves and flowers made with water or wine, *or to apply them as poultices* to the affected parts." This noted astrological physician also commends the water violet—which he denominates a Saturn herb—as "of great use against the king's evil, and all scrofulous swellings."

103. As among a trinity of kingdoms or planes, the animal, the vegetable, and the family of stars are pretty intimately related. The moist consistencies of the two respond most readily to the electro-magnetic vibrations of the third, and in time and degree according to susceptibility and relationship.

tion, is a proof of the diffusion of collateral elements throughout the various channels of expression, and of a constant stream of influences forever interacting between those that stand thus related to each other. "Every metal and very plant possesses certain qualities that may attract corresponding planetary influences, and if we know the influences of the star, the conjunctions of the planets, and the qualities of our drugs, we will know what remedy to give to attract such influences as may act beneficially upon the patient." (Paracelsus.) Modern medical science, resting upon a putative basis, is not only confessedly ignorant of the origin of disease but of the curative action of physic as well. Paracelsus here reveals the gist of the secret.

104. While the modern pharmacologist invents many arbitrary combinations which are in turn blindly prescribed according to the dicta of pure experimentalism, the old-time herbalist based his deductions upon a law of principles cooperative between constitutions cognate in relationship. And no department in nature can be intelligently studied without a conversancy with these similitudes. To correctly apprehend the lower, one must mount the ladder of analogy into the realm of that celestial symbolism wherein reposes the key not only to the mysteries of Man, but to all divine order.

105. The higher the plane of manifestation the more sublimated are the life essences, and therefore the more impressible by astral influx. Thus, the human being is a responsive center to manifold influences of which the plant gives no token; in turn the molecular sensitiveness of the vegetable structure imbues it with the power to perceptibly acknowledge its star, while the metal and the mineral repose in expressionless latency until aroused to action by mechanical manipulation. But no less does a spiritual essence pervade and enliven every form, be it mineral, vegetable or animal, ever making of the higher a compendium of what goes before, and interrelating

The sympathy between plant and planet, so easy of observa-
each with a kindredship that proclaims the oneness of all
nature. Man is an epitome of the whole, a combination of all
the parts, a *quintessentia* of the four elements, a being in whom
the trinity of kingdoms is synthesized into the unity of a god!

106. The mystical worthies who first traversed the space
between the herb kingdom and the stars, knew enough to in-
corporate in their journey a physiology that should not lack in
a single principle essential to a comprehension of the whole,
and thus the botanical and the astronomical were found to
correlate to an exact nicety where the elements in each were
properly understood.

107. In these latter times, however, botany and astronomy
might well be termed the "two orphans" of science, because
of the supine indifference to their lawful import in the family
of Nature. To the votary of the one the irregular branching
of the pedicils of a peduncular tendril is a bliss ecstatic, while
to the devotee of the other a lunar libration which enables the
observer to see approximately 576 out of the 1000 parts of
Moon area, is an eternal rhapsody.

XX

108. Perhaps in no branch of Nature is planetary rule or
interaction so perceptible as in the herb kingdom. Botanical
treatises, without suspecting the real importance of the suggestion, make frequent allusions to the influences of the Sun,

or to the Moon in its waxing and waning, upon certain growths. A little observation along astrological lines would have revealed a more extended analogy in this respect.

Astro-medical herbalism has had some very illustrious disciples, from Hippocrates and Galen up to Culpepper, and to Simmonite, all of whom recognized and taught the important bearing of the astral forces upon the remedial qualities of herbs and plants.

109. While these curative properties as such have never been a matter of question, the irrational and empiric methods in their use as practiced by the legalized pharmaceutist are both inexcusable and deserving of censure. *One cannot proceed contrary to a single natural law without the sacrifice of some specific good which Nature intended.* The question at issue between the modern school and the astro-botanical system which flourished in the age of Avicenna, resolves itself into one of *time* and *circumstance* in the gathering and manipulation of the nature growths to be found in our woods and our fields. The later scientist presumes Nature to be devoid of essential mutations except those which relate to the seasons, and therefore ridicules the fact of constantly varying fluxes in the regions of celestial magnetism.

110. Know that every plant and every herb is constitutionally in sympathy with one of the magnetic planes as indicated by planetary rulership, and that the active period of this rule coincides with the rising or southing of said planet. This fact becomes known through experimentation, coupled with a knowledge of the correlations between these vibratory planes.

111. In speaking of the *rulership* of planets I would not have one infer the power of a greater over a lesser. The Moon does not bring the tide in, any more than the tide impels the Moon to the zenith; the two are but simultaneous interactions of the same occult principle in nature. And so from

the rise and culmination of a planet do we gauge the time at which such principle to which the herb or plant stands related is in most virile activity, for its *magnetic tide,* or inherent virtue, waxes strongest in sympathy with the rise of its attendant star, subsiding again as it wanes from the zenith.

Thus may readily be perceived the rationality of piloting the herbal processes along the currents of this magnet ocean, which flows and ebbs the same as the waters of the sea. Is there, after all, anything so very strange or difficult of acceptance in this fact? To doubt it as a fact is to question the existence of a law of sympathy as the equilibrating force in the universe.

HERBS UNDER SATURN.

Aconite	Darnel	Horsetail	Rush
Amaranthus	Dodder	Ivy-Tree	Saffron, meadow
Barley	Elm-Tree	Jew's Ear	Sawwort
Beet, red	Fern, water	Knapweed	Sciaticawort
Beech-Tree	Fleawort	Knapwort	Service-Tree
Bifoil	Flaxweed	Knotgrass	Shepherdspurse
Birdsfoot	Fumitory	Loosestrife	Sloebush
Bistort	Gall-Oak	Medlar	Solanum
Bluebottle	Gladiole	Moss, ground	Solomon's Seal
Buckshorn Plantain	Gladwin	Mullein	Spleenwort
Buckthorn	Goatherb	Navelwort	Tamarisk
Bugle	Hawkweed	Nightshade	Thornberry
Campion	Heartsease	Parsnip, water	Thoroughleaf
Clown's Woundwort	Hellebore	Poplar	Thrift
Comfrey	Hemlock	Poppy, black	Tutsan
Cross Sciatica	Hemp	Quince-Tree	Violet, water
Crosswort	Henbane	Ragwort	Whortle
Cypress-Tree	Herb Christopher	Root of Scarcity	Willow-Herb
	Holly	Rupturewort	Wood
			Yew

HERBS UNDER JUPITER

Agrimony	Currant-Tree	Hysop	Polypody
Alexander	Dandelion	Jessamine	Rose, hip
Asparagus	Dock	July Flower	Rose, red
Avens, Colewort	Dog's Grass	Liquorice	Rye
Balm	Eglantine	Lime-Tree	Sage, garden
Beet, white	Endive	Lungwort	Scurvygrass
Betony	Fig-Tree	Maple-Tree	Succory
Bilberries	Fir-Tree	Meadowsweet	Sumach
Borage	Goatsbeard	Myrrh	Swallowwort
Chervil	Golden Samphire	Nailwort	Thornapple
Chestnut-Tree	Hartstongue	Oak-Tree	Thoroughwax
Cinquefoil	Houseleek	Ox-Tongue	Wallwort

HERBS UNDER MOON.

Adder's Tongue	Cresses, water	Lilies	Rose, white
Arrach, garden	Cucumbers	Mercury, French	Raggedwort
Awlwort	Dog Rose	Mosswort	Saxifrage
Brank Ursine	Dog's Tooth, violet	Mouse-ear	Soldier, water
Cabbage	Duckweed	Orphine	Spunk
Coleworts	Paverel	Pumpkin	Stonecrop
Chickweed, waterwort	Flag	Poppy, white	Tares
	Fleur-de-lys	Poppy, wild	Turnip
Clary	Molly, sea	Privet	Wallflower
Cleavers	Ladysmock	Purslane	Willow-Tree
Carelwort	Lettuce, garden	Rattlegrass	Wintergreen

HERBS UNDER MARS.

All-Heal
Anemone
Arssmart
Asarabaca
Barberry
Basil
Briony
Brooklime
Butchersbroom
Broom-Rape
Carduus Benedictus
Civet, cotton thistle
Cresses, black
Crowfoot
Cuckoo-Pint
Daffodil, yellow
Dovesfoot
Dragon

Evenweed
Felwort
Flaxweed
Furse-Bush
Galingale
Garlic
Gentian
Germander
Goatsthorn
Ground-Pine
Gum Thistle
Hawthorn
Hedgeweed
Honeysuckle
Hops
Horsetongue
Hyssop, hedge
Lettuce, wild
Lousewort

Lupine
Madder
Masterwort
Mastic Herb
Mustard
Nettles
Onions
Parsley, stone
Peppers
Pilewort
Pine-Tree
Radish
Restharrow
Rhubarb
Rocket
Rosemary, marsh
Saltwort
Samphire

Sanicle
Sarsaparilla
Savine
Sheperdsrod
Simson
Sneezewort
Sowbread
Spurges
Squill, sea onion
Sundew
Tarragon
Thistles
Tobacco
Toothcress
Woodrow
Wormseed
Wormwood

HERBS UNDER SUN.

Angelica
Ash-Tree
Bay-Tree
Burnet
Butter-Bur
Camomile
Celandine
Centaury

Eyebright
Heliotrope
Honewort
Johnswort
Juniper
Lovage
Marigold
Mayweed

Melilot
Mistletoe
Peony
St. Peterswort
Pimpernel
Poppy, yellow
Rice
Rosemary

Rue
Saffron
Tormentil
Trefoil, heart
Vine-Tree
Viper's Bugloss
Wake Robin
Walnut

HERBS UNDER VENUS.

Alkanet
Alehoof
Alder
Arrach, wild
Archangel
Basil
Beans
Bed-Straw
Birch-Tree
Bishop's Weed
Blackberry
Blites
Burdock
Cherry-Tree
Cherry, winter
Chestnuts, earth
Chick-Pease
Columbines
Coltsfoot
Costmary
Cowslips
Cudweed

Daffodil
Daises
Devil's Bit
Dittander
Dittany
Dropwort
Elder
Feverfew
Figwort
Fleabane
Foxglove
Golden Rod
Gooseberry
Gosmore
Ground Ivy
Herb Robert
Herb Truelove
Honewort, slender
Houseleek, water
Karse
Kidneywort

Ladysmantle
Lentils
Mallows
Mew
Mints
Moneywort
Motherwort
Mugwort
Navew
Nep, catmint
Orach
Orchis
Peach-Tree
Pear-Tree
Pennyroyal
Pepperwort
Periwinkle
Piantain
Plums
Poley
Primrose
Ragweed
Raspberry

Rrocket Cress
Rose, damask
Sage, wood
Self-Heal
Shepherdsneedle
Sicklewort
Silverweed
Skirret
Soapwort
Sorrels
Sowthisles
Speedwell
Spinach
Strawberry
Sycamore-Tree
Tansy
Teasel
Throatwort
Thyme
Vervain
Violet
Wheat
Yarrow

HERBS UNDER MERCURY.

Agaric
Bittersweet
Calamint
Carrot
Carraway
Cress, garlic
Dill
Dog's Mercury
Elecampane
Fennel
Fenugreek
Fern, bracken

Flax
Goat's Rue
Haresfoot
Haselnut
Henry, good
Hollyhock
Honeywort
Horehound
Houndstongue
Lavender
Laurel
Lily-of-the-Valley

Licorice
Liverwort
Maidenhair
Mandrake
Marjoram
Mulberry-Tree
Mushroom
Myrtle-Tree
Oats
Parsley, common
Parsnips, cow
Pellitory

Pomegranate-Tree
Quickgrass
Savory
Scabious, lesser
Scorpiongrass
Senna
Smallage
Southernwood
Starwort
Valerian

112. Herbs, as also mineral forms, are natural *vehicula* for the attraction and transmission of such astral elements as are necessary to a restoration of harmony to disorganized physical conditions—a statement which involves the real secret of *how medicines operate*. But in order to penetrate to the magical curative faculty at the center of these nature organizations, it is essential that they be reduced to a state of absolute magnetic purity, that *medicine* and not *poison* be attracted from out the great universal laboratory of the Macrocosm.

113. The importance to the occult chemist of working in harmony with astral law, that thereby the natural and artificial qualities of all things from the Universal to the Particular might be properly attained, may be the better appreciated in this extract from Salmon, an astro-philosopher and physician of the Middle Ages:

"1. The *time* of the preparation ought to sympathize with the native production of the thing to be prepared; which is in respect of qualities manifest or occult.

"2. As to the Manifest Qualities, that time is to be chosen in which they naturally flourish: wherein you are to choose a hot and moist season for dissolution, digestion, and fermentation; a cold time for coagulation; a moist time for distillation and melting; and a dry time for exsiccation and calcining.

"3. As to the Occult Qualities, the preparation is to be begun when the planet governing the thing is strong and vigorous in his house or exaltation, and in good aspect of Sol, Luna, Jupiter, or Venus, or all of them.

"4. The *place* of preparation must be the laboratory, which must be hot, cold, moist, airy, close, etc., according as the nature of the matter to be prepared requires."

The significance of planetary influence, and its relation to the astral potencies involved in all natural operations, is too complex a subject to be fully entered into here, except to say that the truth of the above brief intimations has been amply verified in the writer's experience. Nor when the rationality thereof is once understood, through careful study and investigation of the stellar hypothesis, will one marvel that it should be so.

114. Likewise, in dealing with the spiritual principles of things physical, the Spagyric artist was enabled to perceive the admirable analogies that helped verify the oneness of method throughout the spheres of manifestation, and its identity with those of the Higher or Causative realm, and thereby the necessary interaction and dependence of the one upon the other. Proceeding thus, under the logical assumption that the One Law must express itself similarly upon all planes of activity, they demonstrated the reality of a physical trinity —spagyrically classified as Salt, Sulphur, and Mercury—that corresponded with the Body, Soul, and Spirit of the noumenal world, or the Father, Son, and Holy Ghost of the devotional school; also the fact that these three primal principles embrace and comprehend the four elements, Earth, Fire, Air, and Water, the separation, purification, and inseparable conjunction of which constitute a fifth, of the purest potency, which they termed a Magistery or Quintessence. This on the spiritual plane, as embodied in the esoteric teachings of the ancient religious mystics, is identical with Regeneration, a process the meaning of which churchianity knows as little of as the material scientist does of the above trinity in nature. With this attainment in chemical processes all poison has been eliminated from the matter operated upon, and the spiritual or curative faculty is exalted to the highest degree. The antimonial prescripts of Basil Valentine and the mercurial preparations of Paracelsus were not those which pass to-day as medicines, but which in reality are poisons most dangerous to the vital principle in the physical organism. The alchemists scorned

the use of remedies that yet remained in such imperfect guise.

115. The foregoing hints may be practically illustrated in the following process on the herb pennyroyal, as an example, whereby through proper chemical manipulation the spiritual potencies inherent therein are rehabilitated into a true medicinal form.

Gather pennyroyal when green, and consequently its juices are in full vigor, when Venus is rising or southing, or the Moon be applying to a conjunction, sextile, or trine aspect thereto. Take a great quantity, bruise it well, and putrefy for from three to five days (best done in the wane of the Moon) that the physical bonds be fully broken and the spiritual essences liberated; then mix with it a great quantity of rain water, at least four times the same weight, which distil in a copper alembic; so have you oil and water, which separate, reserving the oil. Take again the same quantity of green pennyroyal, macerate as before, and add to it the former distilled water of pennyroyal, make them ferment with sugar and yeast (two ounces of sugar to twelve ounces of herb), which being completed draw off in an alembic the inflammable spirit mixed with phlegm. This spirit dephlegmate, and likewise reserve. Take the fæces of both parts, calcine them, and with the aforesaid phlegm extract a salt, which purify and volatilize; mix with it the above reserved oil and spirits, and unite them by digestion. So have you the salt, sulphur, and mercury, the body, soul, and spirit, the pure, transparent, and volatile powers—called protestates by Paracelsus—of pennyroyal, having the same smell and taste as the herb growing in the garden.

116. Whereas the apothecary would extract merely an essence with spirit of wine, and discard entirely the fæces wherein is contained the most valuable salts, rain water is here used as the menstruum of nature by which to evolve the natural water of the herb itself. In all instances of digestion and

putrefaction, and more particularly where a quintessence is the end to be attained, a homogene menstruum—as the spirits, phlegm, or water of the subject matter under treatment—is absolutely a requisite, that the astral principles inherent therein be not fatally disturbed, or their efficacy impaired. As saith Paracelsus: "Every fruit must die in that wherein is its life." (*Archidoxies.*) The use of this very word *menstruum* originated in the notion of the old chemists respecting the influence of the Moon in their preparations—a fact sedulously observed, in connection with other astrological requirements, to the end of evolving a perfect, independent microcosm.

XXI

117. The Moon as the earth's satellite claims a distinction not allotted to the other orbs of our solar system. Holding as she does a mediate position in respect of all terrestrial phenomena, she is the chief auxiliary thereto and thus becomes the spouse of the Sun, and so do "all things animate and inanimate sympathize and vary with her."

While her functions as a translator of light is oracularly accepted, there is little comprehension of the method by which she performs this service. When, however, she is viewed alchemically as the moist or feminine principle in Nature one requires but little effort to grasp the fact that she holds in solution, as it were, all the planetary emanations, and that her mutual aspects are but the magnetic stimuli through and by which these astral influences are detached and duly deposited each in its predestinated *locus;* just as an alkali or an acid as a precipitant throws down to the bottom of the vessel any substance in chemical solution. There was crafty logic in the use of the sign Cancer by the old alchemists as a symbol for Dissolution.

118. This moisture of the Moon is the vehicle that affects the conductivity of the astral currents—the insulation that protects the solar wire in its transmission of the fecundative messages. Hence, things of a moist nature respond most readily to the principle she represents, such as the watery element of any organized form; the sap of trees, the juice of herbs, the brain of main, and the very soul of things. As saith Ptolemy: "The Moon principally generates moisture; her proximity to the earth renders her highly capable of exciting damp vapors and of thus operating sensibly upon animal bodies by relaxation and putrefaction."

Which reminds us that a recent article in the *Lancet* draws attention to the moonlight upon putrefactive processes in animal decomposition, to which E. S. Bryant, B. A., B. Sc., in the *Chemical News,* South Africa, contributes a possible explanation. The mystics touched upon the rationale of the same some centuries ago, but from a more occult standpoint, which leads one to suspect there is nothing new under the Moon any more than under the Sun.

119. We have it from Greek writers that hunters, when they sent a boar or a doe to the city some miles distant, drove a brazen nail into the carcass to keep the light of the Moon from tainting the flesh. Moschio, a physician of the time of Euthydenus, affirmed that putrefaction, being a colliquation of the flesh, was more especially produced by the Moon's beams, which carried with them a softening and corrupting quality, and therefore tended to the moisture essential to this process, while the Sun shed a drying rather than a dissolving influence upon flesh. Likewise did Aristotle ascribe

the radical moisture in animals to the Moon, the vital heat to the Sun.

The use of the nail as a deterrent against putrefaction will undoubtedly be looked upon in this enlightened (?) period as a piece of folly or superstition, kindred to many other misunderstood relics of an age when sorcery had its active votaries, and the rationale of magic reposed in the intelligent manipulation of certain subtle laws in nature, termed occult, though no doubt very simple when properly apprehended. Thus, the hunters resorted to the use of the brazen nail because of its astringent properties, a like reason for which the physician made use of the rust of brass, which is known to be "contrary to putrefaction, and healing to corrupting qualities." In this instance the nail but attracted and centered about itself the inhering principle of decomposition. It will now be understood why brass weapons rarely inflict dangerous wounds.

120. It is from this moisture or lunar element in putrefaction that are generated the animal organisms peculiar to putrid states; and similarly the Moon's influence on seed growths, wherein corruption, or the changing of the combining spirit into a moist consistence, is coincident with separation and dissolution, or the processes antecedent to a reorganization of life-forms. And thus why, in Astrology, the Moon is accorded governance over the embryonic period in all fœtal development. As is well known in this science, the watery signs are the most conducive to germination, being termed "propagative signs." The animal embryo is thus nurtured in a sac of water.

121. Plutarch, in Book III of the *Symposiacs*, says: "Even in inanimate bodies the power of the Moon is very evident. Trees that are cut in the full of the Moon carpenters refuse as being soft, by reason of their moisture, subject to corruption; and in the wane, farmers usually thresh their wheat, that being dry it may better endure the flail; for the

corn in the full of the Moon is moist and commonly bruised in threshing. Besides, they say dough will be leavened sooner in the full, for then, though the leaven is scarce proportioned to the meal, yet it rarifies and leavens the lump."

Pliny states (Book II, ch. 41) that accurate observation showed the ant as being very susceptible to the power of this luminary, invariably resting from her labors at the quarterly changes; adding, "and so much the more disgraceful is our ignorance, as every one acknowledges that diseases in the eyes of certain beasts of burden increase and diminish according to the age of the Moon."

122. To the many instances of peculiar sensitiveness to the lunar changes we supplement the following as affording a multiplicity of features worthy of cogitation. Some time ago there was reported in the metropolitan press the case of a young Brooklyn girl of 14, who was designated the "Moon Runaway," because during the year just passed she had disappeared twelve times, once at each New Moon. The astro-student can easily perceive something more than mere pathological interest in these peculiar instances of self-sequestration, how blind soever the family physician may have been to the suggestive correlations: because of the undoubted presence of the pubescent stage (a lunar condition) as verified in the regularity and accordance of the recurrent phenomena with the catamenia, ruled by the Moon. In explanation of these strange vagaries she declared that something in the appearance of the Moon "set her a-going." On the other hand she was often subject to protracted sleep, in one instance sleeping 29 hours, a horary cycle that corresponds to the synodical period of the Moon. Somnambulism had been a habit with her since childhood. We were unable to secure the date of birth because of the parental aversion to any further publicity, but we would like to wager she was born at a syzygy, had the moon rising, or was strongly polarized in Cancer. From

the unusual facts in the case it is not improbable there was a combination of all of these.

123. Aristotle aphoristically states that "no animal dies but in the ebb of the tide," which coincides with the Moon's descension from the meridian. Dr. Mosely recently attempted proof of the theory that the decumbiture of aged people occurred at new or full Moon, seemingly controverted, though exceptions generally prove the rule. It may be observed, however, that all tides, whether of the ocean, of the animal vascular system, or relating to the sap element in vegetable growth, have a close connection with lunar physics, a fact well known not only to the author just quoted, but likewise among his learned contemporaries. Indeed, in the writings of the ancients are evidenced such familiarity and concurrence of opinion in the matter of the Moon's influence upon sublunary natures as should, at least, attract earnest attention to this doctrine, if not conduce to a positive conviction of its rationality.

XXII

124. The paternal character of Hippocrates in connection with the science of medicine has endowed him with an atmosphere of authority naturally endearing to the hearts of his latter-day followers. It is presumable, however, that most of these are but relatively familiar with the more important teachings of this great master, for as a body they seem to have drifted wholly away from the basic doctrine in which reposed the fundamentals of his philosophy. This is chiefly in reference to the art of prognosis, of which latter-day practitioners

are admittedly and wofully ignorant, as judge from the following excerpt from a copy of the London *Medical Press and Circular:*

"Remarkable is the fact that the study of prognostics should be so neglected at the present day, when we reflect how much this department of medical science was cultivated at a very early period in the history of medicine. Some have gone so far as to say that the science of prognosis has advanced but little since the time of Hippocrates; and certainly if we compare its progress with that which has been made in diagnosis, in pathology, and in therapeutics, we must admit that it has been comparatively at a standstill."

125. This writer, whether purposely or not, carefully refrains from any attempt to hypothesize upon this state of affairs, though he might have found the reason abiding very comfortably in the Hippocratic literature, wherein is set forth: "It is the best thing, in my opinion, for a physician to apply himself diligently to the *art of foreknowledge,* for he who is master of this art, and shows himself such among his patients with respect to what is present, past or future . . . will give such proofs of a superior knowledge in what relates to the sick, that the generality of men will commit themselves to that physician without any manner of diffidence."

There can be no question as to the meaning intended to be conveyed in the word "foreknowledge," and the grand desideratum therein implied, for Hippocrates had no hesitancy in declaring that "the man who did not well understand astrology was rather deserving to be called a fool than a physician." The medical scientist of to-day, uninformed of the symbolical correspondence of the heavens with the human economy, is much disposed to attribute this predilection of the master to the proverbial "streak of folly and superstition" believed to be indispensable with a man of genius and character.

I append here an astrological figure culled from my notebook, illustrative of the Hippocratic doctrine of "critical days," for the decumbiture or first seizure in a typhus case that came under my notice. The chart is so arranged as to enable the lay mind in a measure to follow the judgment given thereon. While a figure drawn for the time of falling sick is chiefly for the purpose of prognosis, the testimonies shown are more frequently than otherwise an aid to diagnosis. So it was in this case.

It will be observed that the ascendant is afflicted by Mars in conjunction with the Moon in Libra—a febrile condition

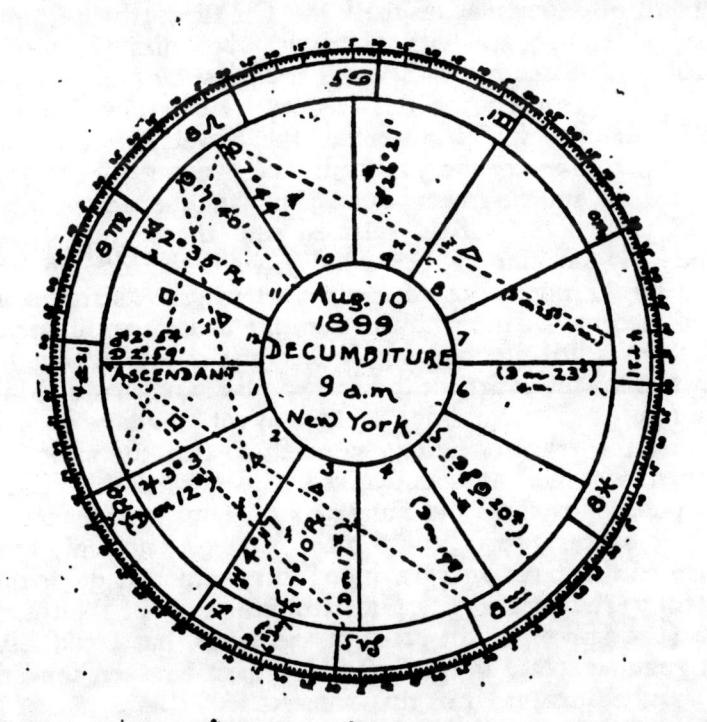

in a nervous sign. The character of the malady is here plainly evident, as the gentleman, after a night of sleeplessnesss and intermittent chills arose with a severe headache (the ascendant governs the head), but his temperature rising alarmingly he returned to his bed at 9 o'clock, the time for which the figure is drawn. Regarding the conjunction above mentioned at the time of decumbiture, Lilly, the noted astrologer of the seventeenth century, wrote: "*Moon in Libra conjunction Mars.—* The patient is grieved with plenitude of blood, and from that cause has high pulse, no rest, is feverish, and an inflammation all over the body. Violent fevers often follow."

The Sun is here also going to an evil aspect, a semi-square (45° apart) of Mars; but as he was supported by a favorable trine (120° apart) with Saturn, who rules the fourth house, or end of the matter, judgment pointed to a favorable termination.

Now let us note the critical days, and see wherein Astrology is a truthful expounder of the law. On the 11th the Moon formed a semi-square with Mercury, who rules the mental activities. The "coma vigil," so characteristic of the disease, was much in evidence on this day, as well as bowel constipation (Mercury in Virgo, ruling the bowels). When the Moon passed the benefic Jupiter in the evening of the 12th an apparent improvement came, but as she immediately squared Venus the patient relapsed into the regular trend. On the early morning of the sixth day, when the Moon passed Saturn (♄), indications of a crisis set in; but as this point is supported by a trine with the Sun, the usual critical period was delayed until the morning of the 17th, at which time the Moon formed the square with her own place and that of Mars in the figure. The condition of the patient was now such as to arouse the gravest anxiety, so much so that the attending physician, who had not familiarized himself with the Hippocratic philosophy, held out absolutely no hope. Any competent astrologer, however, could at the *beginning* not only have anticipated the exceeding gravity of this period, made doubly doubtful by the square with Mars from the cusp of the fourth house (the grave) at the acme of the fever, but could have given genuine solace in the favorable aspect between the Sun (life) and Saturn, ruler of this mansion.

Some troublesome sequelæ naturally resulted, but a palpable subsidence of the fever came on the 19th, with Moon in trine with ascendant and Mars, followed by low heart action on the 20th, with the Moon in opposition of the Sun in Leo (the heart). The crisis on the 23d was not so marked as might have been expected, with Moon opposition of Mars and ascendant. This I ascribed to the fact that the Moon immediately after formed a trine aspect with the benefic Venus, ruler of the figure, which brought a most favorable change, followed by a gradual recovery.

In this example is to be found completely verified a train of preordained incidents. And the Hippocratic doctrine alluded to in these papers rests in the rationality of the law thus cursorily expounded, the full apprehension of which is not to be attained except through the interpretative system of Astrology; hence the reason for the reference made by this philosopher to the incapacity of the physician who is not familiar with astral physics.

126. I am frequently asked to account for the strange alienation of Medicine from Astrology, if, as claimed, the principia of the former is vested in the rationale of the latter. The same question might be propounded in respect to astronomy and to the various theologies, for in the answer to the one is contained the reason for the derelictions of the others.

The explication is to be found in the natural law of cycles (*cyclus*, a circle), in which duality, or the spiritual and the material, is alternately manifested through the two arcs of circular motion designated as centripetal and centrifugal, or the advance and recessional movements in the scheme of eternal progress. As evidences of this statement, take the twenty-four hour measurement as embracing the day and the night; the lunar month with its two periods, that of increase and decrease; the annual solar revolution wherein summer and winter are the positive and negative poles of activity; and, greater still, the precession of the equinoxes, in which the Sun's equatorial passage through one of the signs of the Zodiac constitutes a sub-cycle of 2160 years.

127. The last cycle of this character—in which the equinoctial point receded through Pisces, the sign of the fishes—was completed in 1881. Subtracting from that year the 2160, we have the beginning of the first half or spiritual arc of the

cycle at 279 B. C. This ushered in the Alexandrian and Hellenic schools of philosophy, which dealt with the inhering principles belonging to the eternal and the immutable, and gave to us systems of thought which had to do with cosmology in its comprehensive, spiritual sense; and a little later, on the up-grade of the arc, came the Messianic doctrine, the Christ religion of love and brotherhood, and the declaration of its chief personage that His mission was the fulfillment of the *Law* and the Prophets.

128. Now, as in the daily, the lunar and all cycles whatsoever, this arc comprised one-half of its geometrical value, or 1080 years, which brings us to A. D. 801, where we pass into the recessional or negative half of the cycle. What does the law now disclose to us? The creation of the Holy Roman Empire, A. D. 800, followed by the estrangement between the West and the East; the dislike and the distrust of the grandeur of Greek institutions and Greek culture; the assumption by the church of the dispensing power; the consequent promulgation of doctrines without soul, and the multiplication of dogmas and creeds, each drifting further and further away from the Christ or Nature principle. And from this time forward on the downward cycle, throughout the darkness and the horrors of the Middle Ages, with its feudal cults and their doctrines of forfeiture and eternal damnation, and into the immediate Past from which we are just emerging, Irrationalism, as the outgrowth of man-made ethics, dominated all in its path—science, literature, art, and the reign of creeds almost wholly obscured the sunlight of spiritual truth.

Canst now see the reason for the severance of Medicine from Astrology, the handmaid of Nature and the true interpreter of the Wisdom Religion? And is it any wonder that not Medicine alone, but Astronomy, with the arts and the sciences, should also have bowed their heads in meek servility to the reigning power and have drifted away from the paternal unity in proportion as the circumference receded from the center?

129. An all-wise dispensation, however, bridges over these chasms, generally in the persons of metaphysicians, seers and prophets whose incarnations seem to be for that purpose. Of such were Bacon, Paracelsus, Cardan, Kepler, Lilly, Culpepper, Lieut. Morrison (Zadkiel I.), without whom the most important philosophy of the Egyptians and the Chaldeans, and the teachings of Ptolemy, Aristotle and Hippocrates, would have been entirely swallowed up in the night of Materialism —obliterated by the negative activities of a seemingly adverse law in nature.

130. To the incoming of the new cycle, that of Aquarius, the Sign of the Man, is due the recrudescence of interest in these higher themes, and particularly in Astrology, and I am glad to say that to my certain knowledge a number of physicians are now *secretly* close students of the stellar science.

For the edification of those who are not, the next paper in this series will treat of the logic of cycles in connection with the Hippocratic doctrine of critical days.

XXIII

131. It is unnecessary here to record any of the cumulative instances of expressed hostility of the modern schools of medicine against Astrology. That such has long been their attitude unfortunately cannot be gainsaid—any more than it is of any use to bewail so lamentable a condition. Naturally in this

egoistic age there are many minds minus the power to scrutinize spiritually, minds unversed in the magic art of introspection, and such as are disposed to turn aside from a presentable fact rather than be spoliated of a pet prejudice. But no man nor body of men ever stood obstinately arrayed against truth without in that degree excluding from their spiritual atmosphere the sunlight of illumination. Therefore, the neglect is one which reflects chiefly upon the schools and perhaps is of no consequence to Astrology except in so far as it deprives a suffering humanity of such beneficence as Nature, properly approached, is ever ready to accord her children.

132. That these modern *savans* should continue ignorant of the *fons et origo* of pestilential disease, is therefore not a matter for wonder in view of the limitations thus enforced by a one-sided investigation; for to be persistently enamored of the shadows in nature is to remain ever insensible of the substantial principles whence emanate these simulacra.

133. It is almost incredible, however, that the fact of the periodical tendency of epidemics should not lead them unerringly to the contemplation of regularly recurring causes, such as might logically be looked for in the orderly orbits of the heavenly bodies, and congruous affections so pregnant with divine meaning and suggestion. If these scientific individuals, whose pleasure it is to seek to discredit celestial agency in human affairs, were to observe a man wending his way at stated intervals in a certain direction, and as regularly returning with his pockets filled with gold, I warrant me the acquisitive instincts of said individuals would not for long allow them to remain indifferent to the coincidence. Were they, like the astrologer, but similarly intent with hunger for the wealth of wisdom and a knowledge of the method of God's doing, they could not for long refuse to examine fundamentals, nor fail to catch the melody of Nature's divine synchronals.

134. For purposes of a clearer concept astrologically,

diseases may be classed as of two general types: sporadic, such as are confined to single or scattered instances; and pandemic, or such as are incident to a multitude. The former, primarily induced through stellar contrarieties affecting the individual nativity, has already been touched upon in these papers, together with its rationale. The latter as bearing upon the subject in its more comprehensive aspect, will admit of a treatment doubtless more lucid and credible to the lay mind than is possible when dealing with the complexities of natal astrology.

135. Involved with this aspect of the question is the one of personal liability to pestilential outbreaks, and the fact of scores being drawn into the vortex regardless of horoscopes that are seemingly immune from such attacks. To the superficial thinker along these lines this would seem wholly at variance with the fundamental precept that in the natal scheme must needs be found a presage of every ultimation to which the ego is entitled. Nor is this conjecture opposed to the rules of art, except in its failure to give due importance to universals as distinguished from particulars. As wrote Ptolemy (*Tetrabiblos*, b. i., c. 3), "It is further to be remarked that man is subject not only to events applicable to his own private and individual nature, but also to others arising from general causes . . . since a greater and more powerful agency must of course absorb and overcome one that is more minute and weaker. In great changes, therefore, where a stronger cause predominates, more general affections are put in operation; but affections which attach to one individual solely are excited when his own natural constitution, peculiar to himself, may be overcome by some opposing impulse of the Ambient, however small or faint. And in this point of view it is manifest that all events whatsover, whether general or particular, of which the primary cause is strong and irresistible, and against which no other contrary agency

has sufficient power to interpose, must of necessity be wholly fulfilled."

136. To paraphrase, in every horoscope there exists an affinity for the locality to which said native gravitates. Should that locality, consistent with natural law, become the point of manifestation for the joint action of cosmic and telluric forces—the one of necessity co-ordinating with the other—then every inhabitant as an integral factor in the body politic of such locality is liable to its affections, and the liability is to be inferred from the natural sympathy which constitutes any individual a part of that particular whole. The storm that sweeps everything before it, wreaks celestial vengeance upon a community of interests, nor may the poor wayfarer who bides in its path claim the right of exemption; the boat that carries down with it thrice a hundred souls enacts a law of fulfillment, and the passengers are sacrificed because of the fated sympathy which enrolled their names on the cabin list; while the victims to the malignity of endemical disease but help make up a sum in the problem of a general destiny.

General causes are thus shown to operate in a degree superior to the astral economy of the individual, which in a measure is ever amenable to the environing influence.

Having disposed of this argument, which for long has proven a morsel of rare sapidity to the palate of the sophist, as well as somewhat of a perplexity to the mind of the devoted student, we will proceed to inquire into the *constitutio pestilens* as a concomitant of these same superior causes.

137. The consensus of opinion of medical writers upon the subject strangely converges in the theory of organic impurities in the atmosphere, though being "of the earth earthy," they are too prone to adjudge this condition as primarily due to telluric magnetism. Noah Webster sought to establish a connection between volcanic action and the prevalency of

disease, and while the point assumed is of secondary importance in that it holds a suggestive relation to the minimum sun-spot periods, or times of diminished magnetic fluxions, yet he fails—one might say egregiously—in even attempting an inquiry into the *primary cause* of such action, beyond that afforded by atmospheric pressure. Had he but sought the connection between planetary polarities and the repressive effect of the atmosphere, he would have neared a solution to the problem. But, as with the hard-shelled scientist, he stopped short at this point, doubtless in fear least it lead him dangerously near the environs of Astrology. That volcanic eruption is regulated by electrical conditions in the atmosphere is a fact attested to by the fishermen of the Lipari Islands, who noted the unfailing increase in the vigor of Stromboli during stormy weather; and astro-meteorology has pretty well proven the connection between sidereal and weather phenomena.

138. This fact of a stagnant atmosphere as conducing to pestilential disorders, is well nigh accepted as a universal hypothesis, though our medical worthies, fearful of venturing upon proscribed territory, dare not extend their logic beyond the pale of material contact. Dr. Kilsall, an authority on Asiatic cholera, ascribed that disease to specific miasms engendered by telluric gases; therefore, having made known this fact, it did not further concern him to remember that it is equally the duty of the physician to be able to foretell the recurring periods of so fearful a malady.

139. It is recorded that the "black death," which devastated many countries in the middle of the fourteenth century, was preceded by "stinking mists," and according to a writer in *The Cornhill Magazine*, "Earthquakes were frequent just before the outbreak, and volcanoes assumed unwonted activity. . . . The air over the sea was infected as well as that over the land." Yet this writer was forced to

admit that the cause of this noxious influence was "still a sealed volume." Had it been suggested to him that the causes of these deadly vapors, the earth's eruptions, and the seismic disturbances, were one and identical, and to be found beyond rather than within the earth sphere, his mental equipment would doubtless have suffered a vertigo similar to the terrestrial ones under consideration. He might further have been informed that it is a matter of common knowledge with astral philosophers that a maximum of celestial influx—such as is involved in a series of great conjunctions—ever corresponds with the maximum of virulence in disease. Also in this case the astrologer must take exception to the statement of causes being "a sealed volume"; for just preceding this visitation Saturn and Jupiter were conjoined in Aquarius (an airy sign), followed two years later by a conjunction of Uranus with Jupiter and Saturn, a condition that comports with the judgment of the ancients that the great conjunctions of the planets in the airy triplicity indicate "famine, fierce and violent maladies, and pestilential diseases."

XXIV

140. If no other testimony were needed, the incontrovertible evidence of definite and recurring effects of planetary groupings, such as the one referred to at the close of the last paper, should compel the inference, if not positive conviction, of a well-defined planetary law acting as specific stimuli in the propagation of disease. The archives of Astrology are replete with instances confirmatory of such claim,

but, unlike other branches of investigative effort, the records lie concealed in tomes which seldom meet the public eye.

141. As a few additional examples, I might cite the great epidemic of influenza that swept over Russia and all of Northern Europe in 1782, coincident with Sun square Uranus, Saturn, and Jupiter, at the Vernal Ingress of that year, Jupiter being opposed to Saturn, with Mars opposition Jupiter and Saturn in the month following.

The cholera epidemic of 1816-'17-'18, which affected India chiefly. At the Full Moon in the midsummer of 1817, both luminaries were badly afflicted by the superior planets, these in turn being in mutually evil aspect. Zadkiel refers to the fact that "as these planetary influences lessened, the cholera subsided."

The influenza epidemic of 1830, which practically circled the whole globe. Uranus was opposition of Saturn, 1829-'30; Jupiter conjunction Uranus, 1831-'32; and Jupiter opposition Saturn 1832. There were six eclipses in 1830, phenomena that have ever been regarded by sensible observers as premonitory of earthly ills, as drought, famine and pestilence, according to the positions and afflictions of the celestial indices. There was also an annular eclipse of the Sun in 1831, at which both luminaries were opposed to Saturn. This latter was especialy significant of influenza and of increased mortality.

The cholera epidemic of 1849, which destroyed fourteen thousand one hundred and twenty-five persons in London alone; the visitation also affected Central and Southern Europe. Jupiter was square Uranus, 1847-'48, and conjunction Mars, 1848, while the lunations, eclipses and ingresses of those years furnished additional presages of a pandemic nature.

142. These examples could be extended indefinitely, but it would be only to further corroborate the foregoing; for

adown the centuries, at every instance of pestilence, are to be found testimonies similar to the above, and distinctively characteristic of the particular visitation. It will be observed that Saturn contributes his malignancy to each of the above conditions, a fact not to be wondered at when his rulership of the east wind, which moves contrary in direction to the earth's motion, is taken into account. The east wind conduces to dampness, and a depletion of electricity in the atmosphere.

143. The opinion of Dr. Kelsall that epidemics are due to "some perturbation of the electricity of the earth, either atmospheric or telluric," is a wise middle course to assume, as it is an explanation that in little measure explains. Nevertheless, it is a half-truth, and needs only the tracing of its legitimate relationships with higher causes to arrive at the real solution of the question. Dr. Good, in his "Study of Medicine," was more generous and far-reaching in his hypotheses, for he concedes the probability that "many diseases are influenced by lunations." To medical astrology he rightly ascribes an intimate connection with meteorology, but deplores the fact that "of all the subdivisions of general philosophy there is none so little entitled to the name of science as meteorology." I know not what the meteorologist may think of this artful estimate, but I do know the *astro-meteorologist* heartily agrees with it. The former, however, might give a Roland for the doctor's Oliver by commending to his notice the statement of Liebig—quoted in a former paper—that "medicine as an inductive science occupies the lowest place." An opinion, by the way, in which the astrologer also concurs.

144. To enter as deeply into a discussion of astro-meteorology as would be needful to illustrate its relation to pestilential disorders, would entail a treatment unnecessarily complex for so simple a truth. Periods of storm, earthquake, seismic

disturbance, and other convulsions of nature, are so peculiarly contemporaneous with endemic and sidereal phenomena, that to the open mind the connection between them is too obvious for doubt. Indeed, the fact that disease is largely affected by conditions of the atmosphere is one so generally recognized by medical writers, that this much of the question may not be considered at issue. But this touches on merely an infinitesimal part of the truth, and it yet remains for the modern disciple of medicine to perceive the wondrous mutuality of each with the other, in all their bearings. The extensiveness of the subject, as thus implied, should impress upon his mind the wisdom of Paracelsus in maintaining that the physician should be acquainted with *all* the laws of nature, for, as he averred, medicine rested upon the four pillars of Philosophy, Astronomy, Alchemy and Physical Science.

145. To reconcile the theory of sidereal physics and the effects produced thereby, with the now popularly accepted science of mind, may seem somewhat of a difficult task, though there is naught in the one at which the other might take umbrage. In reality they each involve but different phases of the same truth—that of identity of principle, whatever the plane of manifestation.

146. The metaphysician tells us that disease results chiefly through fear, implanted either consciously or subconsciously in the spiritual organism. But what is Fear other than the active expression of the Saturn principle in the microcosm of nature? This interpretation will be found in any general treatise on the subject of Astrology; and, as indicated above, Saturn is invariably conspicuous as a disturber during pestilential periods, through his crystallizing functions furnishing the stagnant conditions necessary for the engendering of miasms in the physical atmosphere.

147. But Saturn is by no means alone responsible for the chirography on the telluric envelope. Jupiter instills into it

the putrefactive moisture essential to its absorption, while Mars energizes the dire import of the message. Thus, in the grouping together of several planets Nature combines her forces into potentiality, and exerts her whims according to the element that predominates. Is it any wonder that such messages should carry so far and be disseminated so widely?

148. The susceptibility of the individual to infection signifies either the natural response of some element in his astral sphere to the tenser throbbings in the sidereal organism, or else the attraction, from out the greater world, of impulses similar in nature to those actively within. "No evil influence can develop a disease where the germ of that disease does not already exist. If evil elements exist in the sphere of the soul, they attract such astral influences as may develop diseases." (*Paramirum.*) Reference is here doubtless made to *thought* germs, and not to the irresponsible animalculæ that are discussed with such avidity by writers who delight to theorize upon a *contagium vivum* as the fundamental cause of disease. Paracelsus dealt with principles rather than things themselves, with the noumenal rather than the phenomenal, hence the facility with which he probed to the center of truth itself.

149. The germ of fear is more often than not the magnet that "attracts such astral influences as may develop diseases," and this quality of mind comes especially under the dominion of Saturn, who is the killer and not the giver of life. If this sinister element in man could be entirely eliminated, disease would vanish, never more to return. But not until the inner arcana of his being are better understood, will man be able to fortify himself against susceptibilities consequent to his ignorance.

150. If Mars be the dominant factor, martial moods will result, as is generally the case when this planet is in perigee at the same time the earth is between the Sun and Mars—as

during our war with Mexico, the severest period of the Civil War, the Homestead troubles, and the Pittsburg riots; or, when the lunations, ingresses, great conjunctions, or the eclipses, are especially contaminated by his beams. This astral affection induces to antagonisms between the magnetic and electric currents in the earth's aura, and coetaneous disturbances in the thought realms of man; hence, febrile and inflammatory diseases, war, strikes, revolution, and kindred disorder. It has been observed that martial maladies are particularly prevalent in war times, obviously due to the mutual conflicts and turmoils on the emotional planes co-existing with the ascending influence of this star. Other planets beget similarly characteristic effects when so conditioned as to exert a maximum potentiality.

And thus might all phenomena, atmospheric, terrene, mental,—storm, upheaval, pestilence,—be traced unerringly to their rightful source in the cosmic energies, each serving objectively as a demonstration of the universal impingement which constitutes Nature a system of diversities subsisting in the bosom of a SUPREME UNITY.

An Enquiry Concerning Our Nation's Nativity

I doubt if there be any subject of more real vital interest to the student of Judicial Astrology than the birth figure of our Independence. Various ascendants have been assumed, calculated, theorized upon, but we may be pardoned if most of the testimony thus adduced seems to us too indeterminate for the settlement of the problem at issue.

We have in mind an earnest delver in this direction who concluded after long and arduous computations that he was justified in making Virgo a finality in the matter, though the few citations favorable to that sign seemed very meagre in a chronology replete with essential happenings, from the laying of corner-stones to the waging of great battles, and which include in their natii every segment of the zodiacal circle.

In view of such diversity one is necessarily led to infer that any of these various ascendants is but relevant to the character of the particular incident to which it relates, and that the whole of the twelve signs may govern respectively according to the nature of the circumstance. This may be illustrated in the following enumerations, each of which we believe to be of more than passing gravity to the nation at large, and wherein Virgo did not occupy the ascendant.

1. Cornwallis surrendered Oct. 18, 1781, about 9:30 A. M. Leo ascendant.*

*Bancroft's "Life of Washington," p. 288.

2. Washington took the first Presidential oath, April 30, 1789, 0:45 P. M. Sagittarius ascendant.†

3. Emancipation Proclamation signed Jan. 1, 1863, middle of afternoon. Gemini ascendant.‡

4. Cuba declared independent by Congress, April 19, 1898, 2:40 A. M. Aquarius ascendant. An assimilative measure.

5. Ultimatum to Spain signed April 20, 1898, 11:10 A. M. Leo ascendant.

6. Cancer rises March 4, between noon and 1 o'clock, when the Presidential oath is invariably taken.

And so on, *ad infinitum*.

Besides, to reason by analogy, one must admit that many serious moves not conjunctive with the radical ascendant take place in the experience of every individual. At this moment we have in mind an instance in which the last will and testament of a Gemini person was signed when Capricorn, the ruler of the 8th house, was rising; another, where a Leo native threw open the doors of a big wholesale business with Sagittarius culminating; while the horoscope of offspring are quite as often at variance with the ruling signs, and yet one must concede that such events are of paramount importance in every household government.

From these premises the non-utility of this line of evidence must be apparent.

Dr. Pearce's assumption of the Bull's North Horn (B Tauri) as a determining factor in the solution of the problem, was logical in theory if not fruitful of results, for the ancients to whom he hearkened laid great stress on the operations of the fixed stars as being more comprehensive than the planets in their effect on national destiny. To quote from Bonatus:

"The Fixed Stars are most slow in motion, and conse-

† Lossing's "Biography of Washington," vol. II, chap. viii.
‡ "Lincoln and the Emancipation Proclamation," McClure's, April, 1899.

quently in mutation; whence it comes to pass that their impressions require subjects and patients of the same nature, that is to say, such as are the most lasting, and carry a conformity with them to perfect or accomplish their effects.

". . . The significations of the Fixed Stars being so great, so high, and free from mutability, they cannot easily take upon them a variable commixture with things quickly corruptible and suddenly changeable. (Con. 141.)"

Zadkiel I. also inclined to Gemini as ruler of the figure, but the opinion obtains that he was greatly influenced to this through the regency of this sign over North America generally, a fact conceded by astrologers who wrote previously to the Revolutionary period. Sibly's work, published in 1788, gave 19° 49' Aquarius as the probable ascendant, though on what authority this calculation was based deponent sayeth not. With his usual disregard for mathematical accuracy Sibly used a table of houses for London latitude.

A tradition still exists in the New England states to the effect that the bells announced the tidings at cock crow, though this obviously had reference to the local gongs rather than the one of Liberty fame. Besides, methods of communication between such distances at that time would discredit testimony of this character as of any possible value.

First, touching upon the validity of this chart as an astrological basis for our nation's nativity, the argument has been advanced that July 2, which witnessed the Resolution of Independence, was technically the natural moment of birth. But the Resolution and the Declaration were separate and distinct measures[*], and, as embodied in the journal of Congress for July 4, the latter was officially commemorated as "a Declaration by the Representatives of the United States

[*] "Notes on Lord Mahon's History of the American Declaration of Independence," Peter Force, p. 38.

of America in Congress assembled," and so announced to the world. So much on that point.

We have drawn attention to three distinct charts illustrative of the actuating conditions which surrounded this immortal state paper, two of a Mercurial character and one Aquarian. Let us examine cursorily into the respective premises, and see in what measure the testimonies accord with later developments.

In the Sibly chart, Aquarius rising (Pisces intercepted), ours would seem to be a destiny of perpetual opposition, with Saturn and Neptune in the 7th, and Uranus and Mars opposing the Midheaven. These point to a disruptive rather than a constructional tendency, and the stability of our home interests would have been chronically endangered; in contradistinction to which our internal economy was unfolded and fructified with a rapidity surpassing even the phenomenal. A contributive element in favor of the probable accuracy of this chart was the transit of Uranus through its 4th during both the Revolutionary and Civil War periods. In this least important of the four angles it would be a co-operative but relatively an inferior factor as compared with the multitude of other disturbing forces that had to be encompassed ere we became a full-fledged Nation. 10 P. M. on that date—the approximate time postulated as the basis of this world-important happening—seems a pretty sad commentary on the integrity of Astrology as a scientific key to the known facts in the subsequent outworking of our national destiny. We trust no ephemeris annotated thus unoffiically by Sibly has had the misfortune to impose upon the credulity of any later student, as the Philadelphia latitude would give the early degree of Pisces on the ascendant, affording equally as vicious a foundation and such as would measure to about the same degree of mediocrity in unfoldment.

In the Gemini horoscope the ascendant is sadly afflicted

by two malign influences, and instead of a peaceful, law-abiding, and neutrally-inclined community, patient and conservative under trying circumstances, we would have constantly paraded with a chip on our shoulder. In many respects the chart is more significant than the preceding one, for with Venus and Jupiter in the second mansion one might easily have divined the possibilities which have made us a Utopia among nations in point of enterprise and thrift, and that with our full natural resources scarcely drawn upon. But venom and not amity would have characterized our domestic interchanges, instead of which we are a family grown to 48 states, each in close allegiance to the parent stem, and, with the exception of one episode, free of internal wrangling other than such as belongs naturally to the expanding vitality of lusty offsprings.

The Virgo map, with the god Neptune trying to look dignified in the earthy element, votes us a sham, a commonwealth heartily given to double-dealing, and, in addition, with the meridional point so heavily besieged, entirely contradicts the high-minded official integrity which marked the lives of Washington and Lincoln, and, with possibly one or two exceptions, the entire line of our Chief Executives. Saturn on the cusp of the 2d, ruling the 5th, and squaring the Sun, would keep us in a state of speculative bankruptcy, contrary to which United States securities usually maintain a healthy marginal advantage throughout the world's markets. The conjunction of the benefics in the 10th is a factor not to be overlooked, however, in considering the merits of this scheme.

Thus it will be observed that, while indicating the apparent anomalisms in these figures, we seek not to undervalue the consistencies which may be found therein. On the other hand, if one dare not carry a prejudice into the vestibule of Truth, neither will the spirit of enquiry permit the slighting of any testimony, hypothetical or otherwise, which may serve to

Astrosophic Principles

throw light upon a subject under discussion. For which reason we have searched further into this matter, and present herewith a horoscope of the Declaration whose basis is more

HOROSCOPE OF THE DECLARATION OF INDEPENDENCE.

Time, 0:20 P. M. July 4th, 1776.

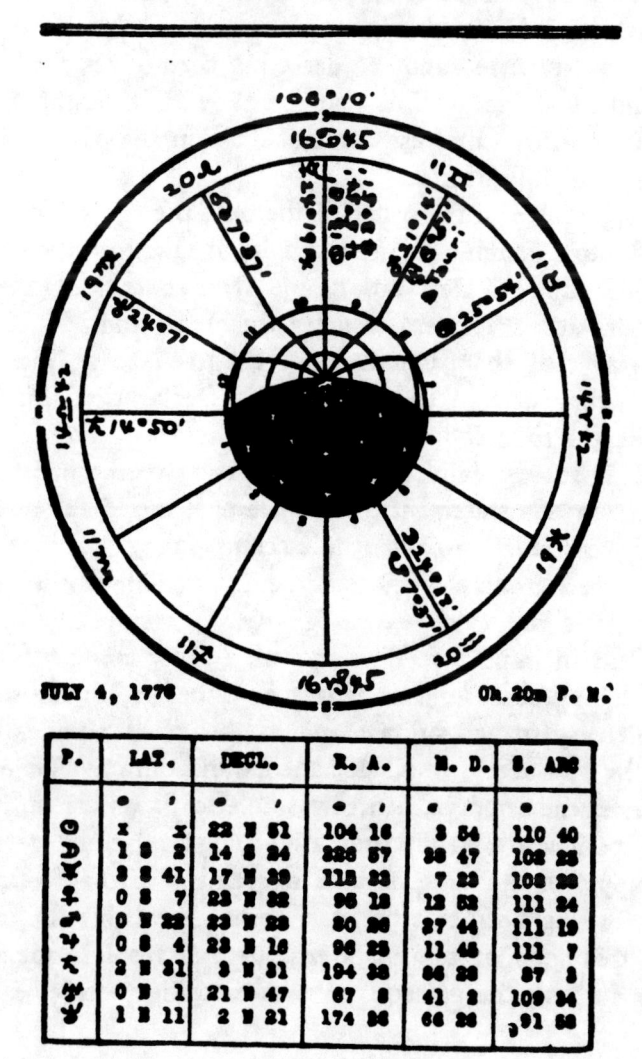

in keeping with historical fact, and whose radical features as well as its directional testimonies seem to approximate more nearly to the real significance of this document, and the marvelous chain of events which it subsequently evolved.

According to Lossing (Harper's Magazine, June, 1851, p. 153), a historian whose work is noted for the quantity and accuracy of its detail, "At a little past meridian, on the Fourth of July, 1776, a unanimous vote of the thirteen colonies was given in favor of declaring themselves free and independent states." This statement owes its authenticity to the Journal of Congress for that day, on the pages of which is also the following:

"Agreeably to the order of the day, the Congress resolved itself into a committee of the whole, to take into their further consideration the Declaration; and *after some time* (the italics are ours) the President resumed the chair, and Mr. Harrison reported that the Committee have agreed to a Declaration, which they desired to report. The Declaration being read, was agreed to as follows: . . ."

This substantially settles all doubt as to the hour of day, and from this statement of "a little past meridian" as a basic factor or starting-point the accompanying rectification is made, the astronomical elements being calculated from Parker's Ephemeris for 1776.

Bear in mind that Lossing was a most conscientious and painstaking searcher into whatever came within the scope of his literary investigations; and in this matter under discussion he had access to all documents and data available in the Government archives, hence was able to fix as conclusively as an experienced and discriminative judgment could determine, the approximate time of final agreement to the Declaration. This having been effected it is neither probable nor credible that this body of unusually zealous and resolute men forthwith forsook the palestra of debate to hie themselves to the gastronomic calmness of the evening meal before affixing their signatures to a message, already agreed upon, that was intended to reach to the furthermost ends of the earth. Instead, it is more than likely that Liberty Bell was proclaiming the glad tidings as soon thereafter as the belfryman could negotiate the distance to the tower whence clanged the first dulcet note of Freedom.

And even had they thus temporized—not a logical supposition—the Agreement was the psychological and determinant step that gave to the act the stamp of finality.

To the student of the stars the reflex of the heavens as here presented is as remarkable in itself as is the unprecedented march of triumph which it foreshadowed, for the spirit of that famous document pulsates and throbs in every element therein revealed.

Cardinal signs on the angles, Venus the ruler of the scheme in conjunction with the benefic Jupiter on the cusp of the midheaven, with Saturn dignified in the eastern angle whence rose this new star of promise, in Libra, the symbol of justice, and in favorable trine aspect to Mars and Uranus in a mercurial vesture in the ninth mansion, and Mercury elevated in sextile to Neptune—all are singularly significant of that prestige we have attained to in the caravan of nations; of our development in the industrial arts and sciences; of our preeminent standing in the world of exact science and natural philosophy; of our initiative in the experimental fields of racial reforms; of our intolerance of those incongruous systems of national polity which can boast a belief in the omnipresence of a just God while yet unable to countenance the fundamental doctrine of human equality.

As might be unthinkingly supposed, the first house of this figure—as in mundane astrology—does not typify the citizenry, except as they are related *en masse* to a comprehensive destiny; their domal quarter is the fifth house. But it does stand as a nationalistic sponsor, while the Libran ascendant, with Saturn therein, is likewise temperamentally reflective of the Signers themselves—deep-thinking, wise-brained, sturdy humanitarians, seeking justice for the unfortunate and the down-trodden, and thus infusing into the very body of that which they had created their own convictions concerning the right to impartial and co-extensive privilege and opportunity. And the nearer a nation approaches to a recognition of the inalienable rights of the individual, the closer must be its affiliation with that universal law whose dictum can neither be abrogated nor perverted by the rulings of an arbitrary method of judicature. The position of Mars and Uranus is ample evidence of the fact that neither conventionalism nor sycophancy could ever have become a part of our social economy, nor sentimentalism the basis of our theories or institutions. We cannot be charged with a paucity of that sort of imagination which devises, invents, and ever provides the means to an end, no matter what sphere of activity be involved; yet nevertheless, we are essentially matter-of-fact.

The student will recognize in the fortifications of the 5th house, occupied by the Moon, an index to the heterogeneous and independent character of our population. Our country's children, native and adopted, are not lacking in the faculty of absorption, nor in the elements of adaptability to new customs and surroundings; and they will sway their own destinies, for they have the ruler of the 10th, the post of honor, in their midst.

It is interesting to note that the sign Leo, ruling France, is on our house of friends. This explains astrologically France's sympathy for us in the incipient period. But in 1861, when we were threatened with dissolution through grave internal complications, the Sun, lord of Leo, had progressed to an evil square of Venus and Jupiter, at which period the Union was not blessed with very pronounced sympathy on the part of allies, and France's attitude toward this Government was rather questionable.

The western angle, our opponents, is governed by Aries, the sheath of Mars, and the ruling sign of England, and we find the significators of the 1st and 7th in antagonistic parallel, but the first in elevation over the latter. Thus the alienation which this document immortalizes is strongly shown in the horoscope. But as the progressed Sun (a dignitary of the 7th) became more centered in our ruling sign this strain, so often perceptible previously, has been practically removed. We trust it will remain so, for the question of progress and civilization logically demands the co-operation of these two peoples, speaking the same tongue, and actuated by the same earnest desire for the upliftment and development of the races.

These pertinencies might be much extended, did space and time permit. We would ask a passing reference, however, to our naval prowess, amply instanced in the sea contests of the past, and in gunnery percentages and strategical superiority in peace times of later years. These are powerfully indicated in the conjunction of the two benefics in the maritime quarter in a watery sign, Jupiter ruling the 6th (the Navy). We would also reiterate the fact that the 10th house sign as sponsor for the highest office in the gift of the people (Moon), ascends at each inaugural ceremony.

Assuming a horoscope of this magnitude to be identical in its methods of unfoldment with the more circumscribed economy of the human ego, we append here a few confirmatory directions in arc, with an abridged table of progressed lunar positions. From the accompanying Speculum the student may carry his investigations further than it has been our privilege to do.

Saturn so close to the ascendant shows many early struggles, being particularly unfortunate in 1777 (Ascendant conj.

Saturn, mundo direct), including the defeat of Washington by Howe, and the capture of Philadelphia.

M. C. conj. Mercury mundo direct, arc 7° 23', a logical influence measuring to the regulation of trade with America by British Council, and the Definitive Treaty with Great Britain in September, 1783, immediately preceded by the peace of Versailles.

Sun conj. Jupiter conv. zod., arc 7° 48', spring of 1784. United States Congress organized and begins its first active duties; great increase in trade and commerce.

Moon trine Venus d. d. zod., arc 10° 16', September, 1786. Convention to establish a general tariff on imports and to regulate commerce (Venus in 9th).

M. C. conj. Jupiter conv. zod., arc 11° 45', May 23, 1788. Constitution ratified.

Moon trine Jupiter d. d. zod., arc 12° 26', November, 1788. Constitution goes into operation, and the first steps taken toward the choice of a Chief Magistrate (Moon ruling 10th).

M. C. conj. Venus mundo conv., arc 12° 52', or April, 1789—the ruler of the figure to the mid-heaven, inauguration of the first President.

Sun conj. Mars conv. zod., arc 13° 46', March, 1790. Discontent among the Indians, extending throughout the western tribes, and followed by open hostilities.

M. C. trine Moon conv. zod., arc 24° 27', fall of 1800. Treaty of Amity and Commerce with France; capital removed to Washington, and the first session of Congress in that city.

M. C. conj. Mars conv. zod., arc 27° 44', March, 1804. Inception of hostilities with the mother country, with periodical agitation, including:

M. C. square Mars d. d. zod., arc 28° 31', interruption of American carrying trade in the early part of 1805; and

M. C. sextile Mars d. d. zod., arc 35° 23', reparation for the *Chesapeake* affair in the fall of 1811; at the same time a recrudescence of our Indian troubles, followed by misunderstandings which developed into a second war with Great Britain.

Sun conj. Uranus conv. zod., arc 37° 34', January, 1814. This year witnessed many national perplexities, hard fighting on land and sea, culminating in the investiture of Washington by the British and the burning of the Capitol.

Asc. opposition Mars d. d. zod., arc 83° 35', winter of 1860. The linking of the Kansas troubles with the outbreak of war.

M. C. conj. Saturn mundo direct, arc 86° 15', or September, 1862. The approach of the meridional point to the body of this malefic coincides with the progress of the Civil War, the repeated reverses of the Union forces, the arc reaching completion when everything seemed darkest for the nation, and just preceding victory at Antietam, which was the keynote for the preliminary proclamation, and the turning point of the Rebellion.

Sun conj. Saturn d. d. zod., arc 88° 24', spring of 1865 by Naibod's measure of time, the last sad scene in the war drama before ringing down of the curtain, in which a martyred hero constituted a fitting apotheosis.

The first two assassinations occurred under a combined influence of Sun with Saturn; at Garfield's assassination the Moon was in Sagittarius, the third house of this chart, and the President was at a railway station starting on a short journey. The Moon was passing through our 7th and 8th houses during our two greatest wars—the points of conflict, death and desolation. The lunar oppositions at the cholera epidemic in 1832 from common signs and the 6th and 12th houses, are also significant. This condition was coincident with Jupiter's approach to the Sun, and was no doubt much intensified thereby, as the perihelia of the planets are invariably accompanied by a vitiation of the atmosphere and a diminution of the solar energy.

Some interesting facts may be observed in the table of secondary and lunar directions (herewith submitted).

DATE	Direc. Moon	Lunar Aspects	Mutual Aspects	Historical Events	
Oct. 18, 1781	8 55 ♉	⚹ ♀ ☿ P		Surrender of Cornwallis.	
Sept. 24, 1782	21 54 "	⚹ ☿ P	☉ ☌ ☿ ℞	Ind. ack. by Great Britain.	
Nov. 30, 1782	24 29 "	⚹ ☿ ℞ ☌ ☉	☉ ☌ ☿ ℞	Provis'l Peace with Gr.Brit'n	
May 23, 1788	5 7 ♌			Constitution ratified.	
Apr. 30, 1789	17 51 "	∥ ☿ ℞	♀ ☌ ☿ P	Inaug. of first President.	
June 18, 1812	23 54 ♊	□ ☿ ℞		War declared with Gr.Britain	
Oct. 19, 1814	23 46 ♋	☌ ☿ ℞ ⚹ ☉	☉ ☌ ♀ P	Surrender to Federal Army.	
April, 1832	7 35 ♓	☍ ☉ P		Cholera Epidemic in U. S.	
June, 1832	10 7	☍ ☿ P			
Sept. 1832	12 39 "	☍ ♀ P			
Sept. 22, 1856	22 3 ♑	□ ♄ ☍ ♃ P		Troubles began in Kansas.	
Sept. 23, 1857	6 5 ♒	☌ ☊		Great Panic.	
June, 1858	16 53	□ ♂ P		Renewed Kansas troubles.	
Dec. 20, 1860	23 57 ♓	☍ ♅	♂ ∥ ☽ ☿	S. Carolina seceded.	War Period through Gemini
Apr. 6-7, 1862	14 22 ♈	□ ☉ ☍ ♄ ℞		Shiloh.	
Aug. 28-30, 1862	19 41 "	☍ ♀ P		Manassas.	
Sept. 17, 1862	20 43	∥ ♄ ℞		Antietam.	
Dec. 11-14, 1862	24 13 "	□ ☿ ℞		Fredericksburg.	
July 1-3, 1863	2 35 ♉	⚹ ♀ ℞ ∥ ♄ P		Gettysburg.	
May 5-7, 1864	15 2 "	150° ♄ ℞		Wilderness.	
May 8-18, 1864	15 26 "	150° ♄ ℞		Spottsylvania.	
June 15-19, 1864	16 51 "	□ ♂ P		Petersburg.	
April 14, 1865	22 24 "	∥ ♂ P	♄ ☌ ♀ ∥ ☉	Lincoln assassinated.	
July 2, 1881	22 11 ♐	☍ ♂ ℞	☉ ☍ ♄ □ ♃ ♃ □ ♄ P ♂ ☌ Cor. ♌	Garfield assassinated.	
April 21, 1898	11 1 ♌	□ ☿ P		War declared with Spain.	
Sept. 1901	21 16 ♍	□ ♂ ℞		McKinley assassinated.	

It is not generally known that there was a Declaration prior to the one under discussion, adopted by the Mecklenburg (Va.) Convention on May 20, 1775, 2 A. M., the text of which was as follows, condensed:

"We . . . do hereby dissolve the political bonds which have connected us to the mother country, and hereby absolve ourselves from allegiance to the British crown. . . . We do hereby declare ourselves a free and independent people . . .

under the control of no power other than that of our God and the general government of the Congress; to the maintenance of which independence we solemnly pledge to each other our mutual co-operation, our lives, our fortunes, and our most sacred honor."

This proceeding was approved by the individual members of Congress, but it was "deemed premature to lay before the House."

From many points of view it would seem illogical to assume the Declaration horoscope to be the official geniture of the United States as a composite body of commonwealths in duly organized form; and therefore as the one essential key to the multiple consortments of the national destiny. True, it was an *avowal* of independence, as the one forementioned, a decisive step towards constitutional liberty—formally proclaiming the postulate of human equality, the validity of certain fundamental principles, and enunciating a doctrine of civil rights as to self-government.

From which it may be likened to the Prenatal Epoch in Astrology, with the subsequent 7-years sanguinary struggle as the gestative regimens (an inchoate period governed loosely under "Articles of Confederation"), and the final organization of the complete fabric into a perfected basis as the true birth and corner-stone of the constitutional structure denominated the United States of America; for "thus the old Confederation came to an end, and the Union began" (November, 1788). Perhaps a specious sort of argument, but the analogy seems rational and sequential, and maintains its appositeness.

Though the testimonies already adduced appear pretty thoroughly to have established the accuracy of the rectification, before leaving the subject I would like to fortify the same by some further evidence, and such as will incidentally suggest an avenue of investigation into the outworking of revolutional figures.

To premise, the conviction is borne in upon one that present systems of determining "times and seasons" are sadly lacking in definite results, and leave many gaps to be filled; and it is reasonable to infer a continuance of the same till the duration of the life-span itself can be ascertained to a mathematical certainty. That fact once infallibly known, many minor periods may then be reckoned in accordance with certain geometric divisions of the individual circle of existence, which must revolve at a rate proportional to its magnitude. For the Law of Necessity demands that said circle be duly completed, whether it be for a day, a month, a year, or longer. I can view this naught otherwise than as a rational hypothesis.

Now, the Solar Revolution—similarly a circle of organized activity—is specifically of this nature, but the directional points in which permit of easier grasp by reason of the normal measurement of time that elapses between the birth and the completion of the annular journey; which is a converse motion of 1° per day (the few days increment in the year may be ignored), or a virtual allotment of one house to each month from time of reckoning. These I would designate as "spheres of influence," each stimulated to activity by the recessional movement of the Ascendant through the domal domains of the chart. The *modus faciendi* is easily illustrated in connection with the Declaration, though lack of space precludes more than a tentative reference thereto. The student who desires to delve more deeply or to seek further possibilities in the method, may do so with his own revolutions, with the reminder that he must (as in nativities) take into account the radical promises in the annual figure.

As examples of this theory, and as further confirmation of the correct time of the Declaration, attention is directed to the following:

SOLAR REVOLUTIONS.

	Date.	Time of Rev.	Ascendant.	Midheaven.
1	July 4, 1860	7.36 p.m.	14.53 Cap.	9 Scorpio
2	July 5, 1862	6.58 a.m.	10.48 Leo.	0 Taurus
3	July 4, 1864	6.45 p.m.	2.33 Cap.	26 Libra
4	July 4, 1881	8.52 p.m.	7.0 Aquar.	28 Scorpio
5	July 4, 1897	5.55 p.m.	28.37 Sag.	12 Libra
6	July 5, 1901	5.19 p.m.	13.16 Sag.	3 Libra
7	July 5, 1912	9. 4 a.m.	5.12 Virgo	1 Gemini

The student is advised to erect the complete figures in order to note the references made, bearing in mind that the 12th corresponds to July, the 11th to August, and so on, as moves the Zodiac from east to west; thus likewise carrying the planets backward 1° per day to body aspects of other planets at time of Revolution, and so in consonance with art. A direct motion at this rate is contrary to reason.

(1) Secession. Mars is rising in this Revolution with Sun opposition Ascendant, and Moon in Aquarius (the Declaration's children) opposed to Saturn, co-ruler of the Independence chart. Internecine difficulties very apparent herein. When the Ascendant entered the 7th, in which Saturn is posited, the legislature of South Carolina ordered the assembling of a convention to consider an ordinance of secession. This was passed December 20th, 169 days following time of Revolution, or when Ascendant had reached opposition Mars therein. This chart was replete with sinister possibilities, which closer scrutiny will discover to the enquiring mind.

(2) Emancipation Proclamation, issued January 1, 1863, just 181 days (degrees) after time of Revolution, which brings the Ascendant to cusp of 7th, occupied by the humane Aquarius (the 5th house of the Declaration). This is undeniably a Uranian force, and could scarcely have been more

in keeping with an act of manumission. The symbolization of 11° Leo rising is "a new Moon," which it certainly meant to the liberated race. The President announced his intention in September to sever the slavery bond; note Venus, ruler of the Declaration figure, in the 10th, corresponding to September period. Jupiter was transiting through the Libran ascendant at this period, thus emphasizing the functions of Justitia.

(3) Lincoln's Assassination, April 14, 1865. The indications are Sun and Venus (ruler of 10th) afflicted by Saturn and Neptune, with Moon, ruler of Declaration 10th, square Mars. The Ascendant had entered the 3rd (April period), where the ominous Neptune was opposed to Saturn. The Dragon's Tail was posited on cusp of 5th (the eighth house from the 10th, and ruling theatres, the scene of the murderous act) opposition Jupiter. Sun conjunction Venus in the 7th was a presage of the close of war, the approach of which became very apparent in December (7th house period) by the complete demoralization of Hood's forces at Nashville—one of the two great armies of the Confederacy.

(4) Garfield's Assassination, July 2, 1881. This occurred two days before the Revolution. The outgoing one being now practically inoperative, the one at hand is given preference. Mars, significator of the President, is conjoined with Saturn (ruler of the July arc) and Neptune in the 3rd (the attack was made in a railway station), and the three afflicting Moon on the cusp or the 8th. The afflicting planets in Taurus very aptly describe the bestiality of the assassin, and their malignant rays to the Moon strongly verify the opinion that he was a victim of obsession or insanity.

(5) Spanish War. Note Mars square Saturn, Uranus, and Venus. The *Maine* was sunk February 15, 1898; Venus in the 5th (February arc) square Mars and opposition Uranus and Saturn, all in explosive signs and the latter two in the surreptitious Scorpio. A mine was undoubtedly planted "with

malice prepense and aforethought." Neptune was in partile conjunction with western horizon. War was declared April 21, 1898, which brings ascendant around to the cusp of Pisces on 3rd (April) in exact trine Mercury in 7th. The Moon conjoined with Jupiter in 9th sextile Sun and Mercury, augured naval supremacy in the contest. Mars was not nicely conditioned for the military, hence the scandal which touched that branch of the service.

(6) **McKinley's Assassination.** This figure is a remarkable verification of the method here advocated as applied to Revolutions. Its radical portents are indicated in ruler of 10th in the 8th, sesquiquadrate Uranus; Sun on cusp of 8th in partile opposition Saturn and inconjunct Uranus, the latter conjoined with the Ascendant, typical of the malcontent who wreaked his vengeance; Dragon's Tail in 5th, or eighth house from the 10th. Now note what happens: President McKinley died from the assassin's bullet on September 14th, 71 days from time of Revolution. This measures in degrees exactly to Uranus conj. M. C. converse, as also to Saturn square Venus conversely over an arc of seventy degrees (days). Could a more apt confirmation of our theory be afforded than in this fulfillment to a day of the event threatened by this Revolution?

(7) I submit this paragraph in illustration of how a revolution foreshadowed the reversal of the national sentiment in the choice of a new Executive. Saturn menaces the meridional point (the Presidential incumbent at the time) by conjunction. Uranus, so frequently inversive of the usual order of things, is in the 5th (children of the country, therefore the voters) in exact opposition Mercury, ruler of the M. C. At time of election Saturn had crept backward to the place of Uranus and opposition Mercury—into a point radically covered by Aquarius; significant in the fact that the Democratic nominee belonged to the Saturn activities of

the Zodiac. What chance had the party in power, if credence is to be given the correctness of this Revolution as based upon the rectification of the Independence horoscope?

By way of emphasis to our conclusions, attention is called to the striking effects of the Saturn-Jupiter conjunctions at intervals of twenty years, the one a co-ruler of the 1st, the other of the 10th. These now occur in the earthy triplicity, the 4th, 8th, and 12th houses of the Independence chart, each of a sinister bearing; and near each recurrence the Nation has been grief-stricken through death of its Chief Magistrate, four having passed out during the term of office under the reign of these conjoined arbiters. Harrison died shortly before the aspect in Capricorn, January, 1842. The next conjunction was in Virgo, October, 1861, the early days of the Civil War, with its attendant carnage and mutations in the body politic of the Nation. The Sun and Mars were in orb of the same point, and at Lincoln's assassination Mars was opposing these places. The next conjunction was in Taurus in April, 1881, and Mars had just passed the point at the beginning of July when Garfield was mortally wounded. The next was in November, 1901, preceded by the assassination of McKinley in September. The deduction is obvious as to the next conjunction, which occurs in April, 1921.

It would be interesting to know how many of the Signers of this document were actual students—not to mention merely the believers—of sidereal philosophy, as the figure itself contains many features of a mystical nature, and is therefore permeated with that spirit. Franklin was a confessed votary, at least of the astro-meteorologic doctrine, as is indicated in "Poor Richard's Almanac." In July (1848) number of *The United States Horoscope*, published in Philadelphia, is found the following: "Thomas Jefferson (to whom credit is given for the original draft of the document).—It may not be generally known that this great patriot and statesman was an astrologer; but let those who doubt the fact examine his library in the capitol at Washington, where will be found most of the standard works on Astrology, with notes in his own hand on the pages."

A volume could be filled with additional testimonies of a pertinent and corroborative character, but such would be only to pile Ossa upon Pelion. We trust, however, the foregoing arguments will serve as an incentive to closer inspection into the merits of the figure as here rectified; for in these generalizations, so seemingly consonant with fact and science, we believe we have approached a step nearer a reasonable and authentic nativity than has hitherto been reached, and though a few minutes' error may exist in our base of calculation, we submit that such need not necessarily invalidate the proximal value of the results thus obtained.

L'Envoi

I was fagged out. The day had been a most difficult one, a cumulative dole of woe that seemed to have left no string unthrummed, no wailing tone ignored. Business perplexity, social intrigue, family distress, bodily ills—all had been duly droned, not to mention the merely trivial though none the less dismal recital of purely imaginary tribulation. Thus doth the noxious, quite as frequently as the joyous, come in "bunches." But the combinations of this day had not been of the sweet-scented variety, redolent of the dews of heaven and sparkling of the sunlight. Quite the reverse.

So when at last I sought my couch much earlier than was my wont, it was to sink laboredly into the "stuff that dreams are made of." But such dreams! far removed from the delightful, laxative fancies that refresh and revitalize the jaded nerves; for instead of contrast to the day's discomfort they quickly resolved themselves into a phantasmagoria that might well have afforded unction to the soul of a Poe or a Doré.

After repeated tossings, and a series of physical gyrations that would have done credit to a worm in lesser misery than that which ached my mind as well as bones, the dream-curtain went up on a blood-red Sun southwest over a plain dotted promiscuously with bleached carcasses, like high lights on a drab canvas, throwing the low places into depths of deeper gloom—truly the remnants of an eighth-house tale that had vanished in the telling. The scene shifted. In its place was to come carnage and bloodshed. I stood on a battlefield, the opposing phalanxes in grizzled front stretching to endless perspectives, armored and helmeted, and visors like unto grinning skulls, from out the hideous openings of which emitted a murky smoke-like substance that seemed the very essence of malice and hatred. Suddenly came commands, sensed rather than heard—a rush—a clash—and the whole became a seething mass so entangled that it was impossible to distinguish friend from foe. The rapidity of the movements of themselves blotted the picture out, and another more gruesome unfolded itself. A pestilence was in progress. People lay stricken in hovels, in streets, and on the open roadways, soon to become fit carrion for the ill-omened birds that hovered above in ravenous expectancy of the provender that awaited them. Then, as one panorama insinuating itself into another, this was replaced by a hall of carousal, the revellers grotesquely costumed, and each wearing a mask fantastically in accord with the perversions of character thus fitly screened: for back of each I saw in the twisted brain convolutions the frenzied germs of a distorted and vaingloried Self!

Thence was the scene sicklied o'er by a gray pall, in the midst of which stood a ghastly skeleton, one bony hand raised aloft and pointing to a lonely Moon moving in a direction contrary to its orbit, and back of which rose a massive Cross, each arm extending to the horizon, and which I took to represent the four angles of the earth. As the Moon descended lower and lower its beams shot athwart a barren field, at the center of which was an open grave, a reminder of the end of things—the conflict of battle—the infection of disease—the banalities of the frivolous and the self-indulgent. I looked more closely. The lunar crescent had arrived at and hung dependent from the nadir of the Cross, and so completed the symbol of Saturn; and I knew the reason for the meanings of the Imum Cœli.

Across the way a church clock broke the stillness. I awoke. It was midnight.

FINIS